It is my sincere desire that the owner of this book would find within the pages healing that only comes from our loving and caring Abba-daddy!

I speak a blessing over your life that you will come to know your Abba-daddy in the full measure of his abiding mercy and power that is available to his children.

Sincerely in His Service,

Your Sister and Your Father's Daughter

Mission of the One Heart Series

To provide milk for the babe, and strong meat for the mature. To rid all who come along on this journey of religious traditions that make us white wash graves full of dead men's bones! So, that we may say as the Apostle Paul: "OH" "That I may know him, and the power of his resurrection, and the fellowship of his sufferings, being made conformable unto his death; if by any means I might attain unto the resurrection of the dead. Not as though I had already attained, either were already perfect: but I follow after, if that I may apprehend that for which also I am apprehended of Christ Jesus. Brethren I count not myself to have apprehended: but this one thing I do, forgetting those things which are behind and reaching forth unto those things which are before, I press toward the mark for the prize of the high calling of God in Christ Jesus. Let us therefore, as many as be perfect (pure in heart, italics mine), be thus minded: and if any thing ye be otherwise minded, God shall reveal even this unto you. Nevertheless, whereto we have already attained, let us walk by the same rule, and let us mind the same thing. Brethren, be followers together of me, and mark them which walks so as ye have us for an ensample. (For many walk, of which I have told you often, and now tell you even weeping, that they are the enemies of the cross of Christ: Whose end is destruction, whose God is their belly, and whose glory is their shame, who mind earthly things.) For our conversation is in heaven; from whence also we look for the Saviour, the Lord Jesus Christ; Who shall change our vile body, that it may be fashioned like unto his glorious body, according to the working whereby he is able to even to subdue all things unto himself. (Philippians 3:10-21, KJV)

our vile body, that it may be fashioned like unto his glorious body, according to the working whereby he is able to even to subdue all things unto himself. (Philippians 3:10-21, KJV)

Notice is hereby given that this author claims the full trademark rights to the all inferences of the "One", the "Heart", and the name "One Heart Series" utilized throughout the various books, tapes and any and all electronic media used to convey the One Heart Series Message.

© 2006, Patricia E. Adams
TM

Copyright © 2003 by Patricia E. Adams

Printed and bound in the United States of America. All rights reserved. No part of this book may be reproduced or transmitted in any form or by any means, electronic or mechanical, including photocopying, recording, or by an information storage and retrieval system -- except by a reviewer who may quote brief passages in a review to be printed in a magazine or newspaper -- without permission in writing from the publisher. For information please contact Shekinah Publishing House, P. O. Box 156423, Fort Worth, Texas 76155, 877/538-1363. Although the author and publisher have made every effort to ensure the accuracy and completeness of information contained in this book, we assume no responsibility for errors, inaccuracies, omissions, or any inconsistency herein. Any slights of people, places, or organizations are unintentional.

Scripture quotations are from the KING JAMES VERSION of the Bible.
Printed in the United States of America

ISBN 0-9700976-1-1
LCCN 99-90786
Journeying to the Road Called Oneness,
An Inductive Study of Intimacy with God

ATTENTION ORGANIZATIONS, HEALING CENTERS, AND SCHOOLS OF SPIRITUAL DEVELOPMENT:

Quantity discounts are available on bulk purchases of this book for educational purposes. Special books or book excerpts can also be created to fit specific needs. For information, please contact Shekinah Publishing House, P.O. Box 156423, Fort Worth, Texas 76155, 1-877/538-1363.

She is a five-fold minister of the Gospel of Jesus Christ. Licensed in 1993 and Ordained in 1996, and serving her local church of The Potters House of Dallas, Texas. She is a Biblical Studies Instructor at The Potters Institute of Dallas, Texas and an author of a series of books on Inductive Bible Study.

The Series is called "One Heart" and cover how to be intimate with God. There are 5 books in this series. God has placed a strong teaching ministry within her spirit that speaks the truth in love, with a commandment to draw his people out and into an intimate relationship with their God.

God has wrought a mighty deliverance in her life from the baggage of physical, sexual, emotional, and religious bondage. Her testimony is that God is a mighty Deliverer and Restorer.

Patricia is available to share her testimony of deliverance and restoration to groups across the country and around the world. Contact her for

- Revival
- Lectures
- Biblical Seminars
- Writing & Publishing Seminars
- Mass Communication Workshops
- Keynote Address
- Family Seminars (Men, Women and Children)
- Ministry of Helps
- Transitional Housing Outreach

One Heart International Ministries
Patricia E. Adams, President & Founder
Website: www.oneheartseries.com
Affiliate Program: www.oneheartseriesaffiliates.com
Radio Network: www.oneheartsoundmedianetwork.com
Email: author@oneheartseries.com

This book is dedicated to My Many Mothers -
   Winnie
   Rosie M.[1]
   Marjorie
   Tommie
   Pinkie
   Verma
   Merlee
   Rosie M.

It has taken many years to realize that because I did not have my biological mother that I was missing out. Recently, one of those that I was closest to and greatly impacted by went HOME and received her reward. And it was then that I realized that I was truly blessed and to be envied that God would bless me with so many mothers, but most of all that I have been influenced by all of them. Not all of them have been kind, but God! And I won't say which ones were mean and which ones were not. Today I know that what the enemy meant for evil, God took it and turned it into my good!

---

[1] It is not a typographical error. My first mother's last name began with an "M." and the last one mentioned her name too began with an "M."

ACKNOWLEDGMENTS

First and foremost I thank my "Lord and Savior" for the life experiences and revelation of the truth of His word concerning the trials that have tried me in the fire, and to the enemies of the light of the gospel of Jesus Christ! It is because of these fiery trials and those enemies that this work was accomplished.

To my son, without your understanding and support this work would not have been possible. It is a joy and pleasure being your mother. Much loves to you my Precious!

And to God, who for many nights and early mornings called me into His presence and drew Rhema understanding of why so much pain and suffering had entered my life. He laid the solution before me, and asked me to apply it to the bitterness and pain of the aftershock of what had transpired in my life. For this there is no other that can take the place of Jesus Christ the Lover of My Soul!

We also wish to express special gratitude to the students who attended the initial Bible Study Training. Thank you for your faithfulness in drawing the Word of God out of my belly, and producing a river of living water within me. To Pastor Phillip P. Brown, Sr. and his Wife; Associate Pastor Ethel Brown, for their divine patience in allowing us to bring this material forth in a church bible study for 4 years.

A special appreciation to Pa-Pa and Mother Dear and Aunt Merlee for being there when needed the most. To Momma Tommie, Aunt Margie, Michele, Margie, and Junliah for coming alongside in their diverse ways.

Introduction

Foundation Scripture:

"And the very God of peace sanctify you wholly; and I pray God your whole spirit and soul and body be preserved blameless unto the coming of our Lord Jesus Christ. Faithful is he that calleth you, who also will do it."

(I Thessalonians 5:23)

Now unto him that is able to keep you from falling, and to present you faultless before the presence of his glory with exceeding joy. To the only wise God our Saviour, be glory and majesty, dominion and power, both now and ever. Amen.

"What is man that though art mindful of him; the Bible records. Man is a tripartite being created in the image of God as an expression of God. The divine plan of God for his created man was that he would love Him with all of himself. This created being would have an absolute desire to fellowship with his creator; from an undivided heart.

Man was created to fulfill the purpose of God in the earth; that is to commune and glory in the benefits of God. The Word of God was the creative force that formed the heavens and the earth, and he alone holds the patent on his creation and the keys to the kingdom. Through the disobedience of one man,

Adam; Satan gained legal access, permission to become the Prince of the Air, but not the Ruler of all the earth.

The Bible says that the earth is the Lords and the fullness thereof, and those that dwell within. Ownership has been Gods all alone!

A song was written that said "…What Satan said was his, has been ours all alone…"

Now, Saints Jesus Christ has completed the work that his father sent him to do, and nothing else is required or shall be done. It is finished! Therefore, we should not allow Satan to continue to deceive ourselves into giving away our authority.

If you do not give him access, he can not come in!

Jesus removed Satan's rights to entangle all areas of our lives through the plan of salvation, He restored us to our original posture in God. Yet, we perish because of a lack of knowledge of the provisions of salvation. Especially, when we protect the painful wounds and fearful memories of our lives from God's healing touch. We literally allow a legal playground to be built, played on, and ruled over by Satan and his imps.

When we receive the Holy Spirit into our hearts, he brings in the entire five-fold ministry tools to run a revival in our dead spirit. The Holy Spirit empowers us to operate as God had originally planned. He lifts us from the ashes of despair!

Ashes are used to speak figuratively in the Bible to express the total destruction of a captive city. Ashes are known to be easily scattered, perishable, and, therefore, worthless. For example, when Satan held us as sinners; we were his captive cities.

But when the Power of the Word, the Blood of Jesus and the Fire of the Holy Spirit destroyed, and stripped bare the stronghold, the threat, the penalty and the sting of sin – we were made free! When something is made it is customized to fit the owner. Those strongholds can no longer rule over us, unless we allow them to!

From that landmark of despair, God becomes our Master (Adonai), Owner and Lord. Symbolizing the authority of God and the covenant relationship from the beginning of creation until the ascension of Jesus Christ. Picture an organizational chart, and the Trinity is aligned across the Top; and in a connecting line the second row links and aligns with the first row. This is what the Trinity has done; it has included those who believe with the authority to sit in heavenly places. We are heirs, co-equals with the inheritance of Jesus. Remember the Bible records that, "The Lord said unto my Lord, "Sit thou at my right hand, until I make thine enemies thy footstool." (Psalms 110:1)

In Malachi 4:3, it says that to the Righteous, the wicked

deeds of Satan are the "...ashes under the soles of our feet." Not that we are anything in ourselves, but Christ within us is our all. Jesus Christ, the Hope of Glory, Gods' Son and His Anointing took on himself our infirmities, and bore our sicknesses.

If you can envision the Lamb of God as He went to Calvary! Carrying the weight and burden of mans' sinful FLESH, the stinch of disease and the full penalty of sin and it's consequences. There on the cross God laid upon Him the iniquities, and the wages of sin that had separated and broken our fellowship with God. Now as the children of God we partake of that sacrificial lamb, Jesus Christ. Jesus said that he would not drink again, of the cup; or eat of this bread of remembrance until he ascended into heaven.

He has ascended and destroyed the wage of sin, which was death! Hebrews 2:14, states that Satan's stronghold was destroyed and those who had been held in hell through fear of death who were all their lifetime subject to bondage were released. Through Jesus' death, burial, resurrection and ascension there is deliverance for us today! We have now been settled and grounded in Jesus Christ and His Anointing. As we are continuously filled with the Holy Spirit, enabled or rather empowered to remain steadfast and unmovable, like trees that are planted by the rivers of living water.

Reflection

"Just because someone did not or does not love you the way that you think they should, doesn't mean they don't love you with all they have."

We all know someone, or have known someone or persons who have not loved us as we hoped they would. Whether they were biological, or intimate, or you were victimized by both. They only gave you what they had, but now it is time to move past what they did not have to give us and give ourselves what we deserve! Freedom from carrying around the dead weight of the people who have left us feeling empty and neglected and move into position to receive love from one who can love us to the maximum capacity of what we have made room to receive. Spring (deliverance) is in the air friends, in the natural and the spirit, while we spring clean our houses, garages and offices, how about the clutter in our souls. Just by faith, not by feeling release those who have hurt you in the past and the present from a debt they can not pay, the check you are waiting to cash will bounce anyway, because remember they can not give you what they don't have. Be free in the matchless and marvelous name of the lover of your soul Jesus Christ!" Again, may you find restoration and wholeness on every page for your life!

Your Sister in His Service Until He Shouts!

Objective In: Journeying to the Road Called Oneness & Psalms 119

- To become transparent before God, the World and ourselves.
- To strip the superficiality of our souls and bare all in the presence of God.
- To embrace the pureness of God's love for us and allow it to purify us wholly.
- To confess the greatest need in our lives are to receive validation and to receive that validation from the only one who can give it unconditionally; that is God!
- We will examine the seeds of toxic emotions that have been planted in our souls as a result of the fall, the choices and the paths we have taken.
- To permanently replace the toxic seeds that have poisoned our past, present and threatens our future.
- Again, may you find restoration and wholeness on every page of this book for your life!

On This Journey We Meditate on Psalms 119

Psalms 119:1-20 Speaks of Correction & Surrender

¹ Happy are all who perfectly follow the laws of God. ² Happy are all who search for God and always do his will, ³ rejecting compromise with evil and walking only in his paths. ⁴ You have given us your laws to obey-- ⁵ oh, how I want to follow them consistently. ⁶ Then I will not be disgraced, for I will have a clean record. ⁷ After you have corrected me, I will thank you by living as I should! ⁸ I *will* obey! Oh, don't forsake me and let me slip back into sin again.

⁹ How can a young man stay pure? By reading your Word and following its rules. ¹⁰ I have tried my best to find you--don't let me wander off from your instructions. ¹¹ I have thought much about your words and stored them in my heart so that they would hold me back from sin. ¹² Blessed Lord, teach me your rules. ¹³ I have recited your laws ¹⁴ and rejoiced in them more than in riches. ¹⁵ I will meditate upon them and give them my full respect. ¹⁶ I will delight in them and not forget them. ¹⁷ Bless me with life so that I can continue to obey you. ¹⁸ Open my eyes to see wonderful things in your Word. ¹⁹ I am but a pilgrim here on earth: how I need a map--and your commands are my chart and guide. ²⁰ I long for your instructions more than I can tell.

Psalms 119:21-35 Speaks of Obedience & Humility

²¹ You rebuke those cursed proud ones who refuse your commands-- ²² don't let them scorn me for obeying you. ²³ For even princes sit and talk against me, but I will continue in your plans. ²⁴ Your laws are both my light and my counselors.

²⁵ I am completely discouraged--I lie in the dust. Revive me by your Word. ²⁶ I told you my plans and you replied. Now give me your instructions. ²⁷ Make me understand what you want; for then I shall see your miracles.

²⁸ I weep with grief; my heart is heavy with sorrow; encourage and cheer me with your words. ²⁹,³⁰ Keep me far from every wrong; help me, undeserving as I am, to obey your laws, for I have chosen to do right. ³¹ I cling to your commands and follow them as closely as I can. Lord, don't let me make a mess of things. ³² If you will only help me to want your will, then I will follow your laws even more closely. ³³,³⁴ Just tell me what to do and I will do it, Lord. As long as I live I'll wholeheartedly obey. ³⁵ Make me walk along the right paths, for I know how delightful they really are.

Psalms 119:1-35 (TLB)

Table of Contents

ACKNOWLEDGMENTS 8
ACKNOWLEDGMENTS 8
Introduction 9
Objective In: Journeying to the Road Called Oneness & Psalms 119 15
1- Drawing Nigh 25
    Intentional with God 27
    Stronghold Breaking Prayer 37
    Lets' Get Dressed -Ephesians 6 40
2- It Is My Life! 43
    Conceptionally Influenced! 43
    Assume the Position 49
    Your Journey 50
    Time! 53
    A Way of Escape 57
    Pursuit of Gods' Divine Success 58
    Reading of the Wills 62
    In the Footsteps of Jesus 67
    Seeking His Face 70
3- Christian: Walk This Way 79
    This is the Way 84
    Come Away With Me 86
4- Christian, What Hinders You? 91
    ANGER: Word Study 91
    Ire 92
    Rage 92
    Fury 92
    Indignation 92
    Wrath 92
    Impatience 97
    Love and Hate 100
    Hatred 100
    Colors of Love 103
    Hatred of - Miso 104
    Hatred of knowledge - Misology 104
    Hatred of Mankind - Misanthrope 104
    Hatred of Men - Misandrist 104
    Hatred of Women - Misogyny 105
    Hatred of Children - Misopedia 105
    Hatred of Marriage - Misogamy 105
    In Summary of Hatred 105
    In Summary of Love 107

    Abuse - Abnormal Use 107
    Self-Love - Narcissism 108
    Emotional 109
    Post Traumatic Stress 112
    Symphony "Sumphonos" 114
    Journey 115
    Trans - 116
5- Y-Intersection 123
    For Length of Days 125
    Measured 125
6 – Our Compass (God's Hands) 129
    Power 129
    Pleasure 129
    Hold Us 130
    Embrace Us 130
    Sheep or Goat 130
    Seated 130
    Standing Up 130
    Exalted/Promotion 131
    Length of Life 131
    Which Hand Do We Choose? 132
7 – Let: Word Study 135
8 – Overcomers to the Right 141
    He Chose Us Over Joy 142
    Have a Seat Over All Things 143
    He Went Down To Get Us and Up to Seat Us 144
9 – When He Said Pursue, Did We Pursue? 149
    Sheep or Goat 150
10 – Oh, Grow Up! 153
    *The Sleight of Men: 153
    Eviction Time 154
    Assignment 154
    React 155
    Relate 155
    Respond 155
11- How to Make Room for One More 159
12 – Now What 169
    Changing the Guard 169
    He becomes our Guide 171
    He becomes our Controller 171
    He becomes our Operator 171
    He becomes our Reprover 171
    He becomes our Life Giver 171
    He becomes our Truth 172
    He becomes our Comforter 172
    He becomes our Teacher 172

- Covenanting With God - (Submission) 172
- Self-Crucifixion - Out With the Old 173
- Gethsemane 174
- Garden of Pressed Oil 175
- Justification - Spring Cleaning the Attic 175
- Regeneration - Remodeling the Attic 178
- Sanctification - Disinfecting the House 179

Enlarging Your Tent 181
- (Obedience) 181
- Enlarging Your Tent Prayer - (Isaiah 64: 1-12) 184
- Cleansed and Salted - Ezekiel 16:4 186

13 – Through Sanctification – Jehovah M'Kaddesh 189

Endnotes 193

Other Volumes in the One Heart Series 194

💜 WHICH WAY SHOULD I GO?

💜 THE BIBLE SAYS THERE IS A WAY THAT SEEMETH RIGHT?

💜 BUT THE END THEREOF IS DESTRUCTION!

💜 FOLLOW ALONG AND LET US FOLLOW AFTER CHRIST!

NOW LET'S TAKE A LOOK AT SOME ROADS WE HAVE JOURNEYED!

CHAPTER 1

♥

Drawing Nigh

"In whatever you do, strive to do it so well that no man living, and no man dead, and no man yet to be born can do it better."
Benjamin E. Mays

Drawing Nigh

1- Drawing Nigh

Requires a heart that desires to follow after God as in Psalms 119; being full of purpose with the intent to accomplish, attain, design, aim, end, object, objective, or goal to complete only the purpose of God in the earth! Seeking the face of God and not the hand of God will bring you to the place of heir and seated in heavenly places! In Volume I; we examined the Plan of Salvation that God has for us so that we would no longer be tossed to and fro by every wind and doctrine. The cover colors were red, black, gold and white - Red was for the blood, black for the penalty of sin, gold for the divinity of God and white for the righteousness we have obtained through Jesus Christ. The cover of Volume II; is blue, black, white and gold. Blue for the priesthood, black for the penalty of sin, white for the robes being washed in the blood of the lamb, and gold for the refiners fire!

In Volume II we want to stay at the right hand of God, because this is how our salvation is maintained. Jesus is seated at the right hand of the Father, as intercessor, advocate and high priest because he became our salvation! Moses understood by faith before the indwelling of the Holy Spirit was given to bring about revelation as we have today; that when God brought them out of Egypt he sang a song proclaiming seven things the saving arm of God was to them as strength, song, salvation, strong deliverer, Father, man of war and Jehovah in Exodus 15: 1-19, I will excerpt a portion here "Then sang Moses and the children of Israel this song unto the Lord, for he hath triumphed gloriously: the horse and his rider hath he thrown into the sea. The Lord is my strength and my song, and he is become my salvation: he is my God, and I will prepare him an habitation; my father's God, and I will exalt him. The Lord is a man of war: The Lord is his name. Pharoah's chariots and his host hath he cast into the sea: his chosen captains also are drowned in the Red sea. The depths have covered them: they sank ito the bottom as a stone. **Thy right hand**, O Lord, become glorious in power: thy right hand, O Lord, hath dashed in pieces the enemy…thou stretchedst out thy right hand, the earth swallowed them…thou shalt bring them in, and plant them in the mountain of thine inheritance, in the place, O Lord, which thou hast made for thee to dwell in, in the Sanctuary, O Lord which thy hands have established." Today God is all of that and some more! We must realize that when we were sinners we worked hard at it! There are 17 works of the flesh and only 9 fruits of the spirit! The believer works less, because the work has already been done, and it is not by works that we are saved but by faith! We are tilling the soil that was broken up "the fallow ground" in Volume I, and *now we are looking for stones, roots and stumps, seeds and anything that would be deposited in the soil to prevent us from receiving* the engrafted and implanted seed of the Word of God into our hearts so that we may grow into mature sons and daughters of the most high God! No longer sucking the bottle, breast or drinking milk from a cup, but we are about to eat meat until we can handle strong meat! Working those utensils and our incisors, eating the whole loaf - the bitter and the sweet! How do we proceed to draw nigh to God! We must be intentional! When you are in relationship with another human being you intend to be there or else you would not be there. No matter what level or intensity the relationship is based on, you intend to be there until you no longer feel a reason to be there or that it is no longer beneficial for you! God says if you would draw nigh to him, that he would draw nigh to you in James 4:8.

Intentional with God

Intention – implies little more than what one has in mind to do or bring about

Intent – suggests clearer formulation or greater deliberateness.

Purpose – suggests a more settled determination or more resolution.

Design – implies a more carefully calculated plan and carefully ordered details and sometimes scheming.

Aim – adds implications of effort clearly directed toward attaining or accomplishing.

End – stresses the intended effect of action often in distinction or contrast to the action or means as such.

Object – may equal end but more often applies to a more individually determined wish or need.

Objective – implies something tangible and immediately attainable.

Goal – suggests something attained only by prolonged effort and hardship.

Our Father wants us to be full of purpose and doing nothing half-heartedly and lax. Plan to be refreshed, restored and blessed! Like an arrow hitting a bulls-eye dead center is what God showed me we are to be in the earth!

The eyes of my understanding were enlightened, when God took me through the passage of Philippians 3:9-11 "...And be found in him, not having *__mine own righteousness__*, which is of the law, but that which is through the faith of Christ, the righteousness which *__is of God by faith__*; That I may know him, and the power of his ressurection, and the fellowship of his sufferings, **being made conformable** unto his death; if by any means I might attain unto the resurrection of the dead." That to draw nigh to him I would have to suffer before I would reign with him! This is just a sampling of the path he traveled after his birth! Placed in ( ) meaning of names I believe are indicative of his journey and the things and levels of conflict he faced.

He had to make a decision to do his Fathers will and this is symbolized by the Baptism in the Jordan (place of decision). He had to submit his self under the mighty hand of God in the wilderness temptation in Jude, so that he would be able to resist the Devil and have him to flee! He received the anointing to make disciples of John and the others in Bethany (house of depression). Because he allowed God to discipline his flesh and gain an overcoming testimony. He was then enabled with power from on High to begin forming miracles in Cana, and participate in his first passover as the paschal lamb (spotless) and could exercise authority to cleanse the Temple in Jerusalem (dwelling of peace). The passing of the baton completely from John the Baptist as his ministry was coming to a close when John was arrested in Aenon (springs). Jesus begins to allow the virtue in him to be drawn out at Jacob's Well and Sychar (shoulder or ridge) in Samaria (watch/mountain) with the woman at the well, he returns to Galilee (central place of comfort) to preach a message of repentance; heals Centurions' Solider in Capernaum (Village of Nahum, compassionate), then rejected by his own in Nazareth (Germ, despised), places a call upon the lives of the fisherman in Capernaum, takes sabbath in Capernaum, goes on his first Tour of Galilee, begins to perform greater miracles by healing of Leper in Galilee, the Paralytic in Capernaum; continues to call out for disciples by choosing Matthew at Sea of Galilee, speaks of the three Parables of Fasting at the Seaside of Galilee, and the journey continues until his ascencion!

    To walk in his footsteps we will find that many of us are walking as he walked and some of us are stuck between assignments right now, you will go through the places of depression, you will be rejected, persecuted, betrayed, lied on, abandoned, you will have a little comfort, you will go through some germ infested places, get to go through some peaceful times, only to be pressed and crushed later, but in order to move on you must complete and pass the assignment you are on! It is all a part of refinement until he can see his reflection in you! This is the process of Salvation after the Gift of Salvation has been received; we are broken and given and broken some more!

One of the most exciting moments recorded in Jesus' life for me is when he proclaimed "No man taketh it from me, but I lay it down of myself. I have power to lay it down, and I have power to take it again. This commandment have I received of my Father." This is powerful he had a commandment from God to be empowerd to lay down his life and pick it back up at the appointed time! To get there we must desire to move out and into the power of God that has been richly bestowed upon us!

Excerpting Luke 8:11-21 "Now the parable is this: The seed is the word of God. Those by the way side are they that hear, then cometh the devil, and taketh away the word out of their hearts, lest they should believe and be saved....on the rock...hear....receive with joy...have no root...a while believe...in time...fall away...thorns are they...go forth, and are choked with cares and riches and pleasures of this life...no fruit to perfection...good ground...an honest and good heart, keep it, bring forth fruit with patience."

The life of a wandering christian is spoken of in Ecclesiates, as one running up and down the street looking for the one who is standing at the altar waiting with open arms, but we are looking in the wrong places and faces! Wandering results from a lack of understanding, knowledge, pursuit of wrong things, wrong people and having wrong motives. Failing to acknowledge the place of rest in the Temple since crossing into the Promised Land. The Songs of Solomon speaks of rest from wandering, because there is sufficient love that will allow us to act on the knowledge of Jesus, and to go in pursuit of Christ and being apprehended of Him, our desires become his desires, and the things we want are in alignment with his perfect will and we receive his supreme blessing on our choices!

When we initially go in pursuit of him we have a love and zeal that makes us yearn for a spiritual life of holiness and to experience him personally, all seems to go so smoothly, trouble free and then the test for endurance begins to bring about strength, durability, and commitment through fires that prove us and refine us and require sacrifices to be made of our own desires and lusts at the altar of our hearts! We are at the we must let nothing separate us from the love of God stage, is what I like to call it!

Our longings should intensify, to be touched by him, the mere absence of his touch makes us want to draw nigh! We are moving past being the sinner saved by grace and into the believer clothed and transformed into righteousness. Moving beyond needing Him and desiring Him, and becoming satisfied with him, wanting to go deeper into the relationship, so we can see duration down the road, and a desire to give him your all and to let him have total access to all of you!

The soul is full of negative complexes, the mind with its vain imaginings and the emotional havoc they all bring. Our spirit receives salvation and we experience the soul and the spirit in the body! Our fears express themselves in doubt, timidity, pride, haughtiness, inferiority, indecision, superstition, cowardice, depression, worry and anxiety.

Reference Scriptures:

Matthew 21:21, II Timothy 1:7, Proverbs 16:18, James 1:5-8, Mark 6:16, I Samuel 17:24, Jonah 4:8, Luke 12:29-32, Jeremiah 32:17, 27, Psalm 32:7, Isaiah 26:3, I Peter 5:7 and Philippians 4:6-7.

How do we deal with fear, since it does not come from God it has torment according to II Timothy 1:7, we must love as he has loved us! Because love cast out fear (perfected love) and we must seek God's control and not ours according to Psalms 34:4. We must learn to rest in God and trust in his goodness and mercy. Fear is unbelief and unbelief is sin. God can and will free us when we confess our fear to him and trust him to be who he says he is. I Am that I am!

Reference Scripture:

Exodus 14:13-14, Psalms 27:1, Isaiah 26:3-4, Matthew 10:26 and Hebrews 13:5-6.

Now we must begin our journey to become one! The spirit of the Lord directed me in 1989 to draw closer to Him, and he would draw closer to me and healing would come into my life. For three mornings straight at 3 a.m. I was awakened to write down this revelation - not fully understanding the purpose God had for me or it! In 1991 he began to call that word forth from within me, after I had gone through a period of backsliding in 1990! He began to build and expand on what he had given me in 1989, and this is when I learned that gifts and callings are without repentance! You don't cease to be what God has ordained you to be when you backslide, you just become a perversion of the genuine article! He restores, reconciles and recompenses you as if you had never left when you return with a contrite heart and a humble spirit! The final interpretaton of this word was confirmed in I Thessalonians 5:23. And the message of the Lord to his people this hour that I have been commanded to tell His people is to become ONE! If you are tired of that sinking feeling and emptiness, tossed emotions and past relationships haunting your present and hindering your future. Then God has the answer; intentionally come after Him, pursue Him, woo Him and he will draw nigh to you! The intent of the One Heart Series™ is to cause you to Love the Lord thy God with all thy heart, and with all thy soul, and with all thy mind." (Matthew 22:37) Through the many broken issues of your life God is speaking to your heart! Can you hear him, probably not, if your heart is broken, heavy and divided into many separate pieces. The Bible states that a house divided against itself cannot stand! Until you have undergone renovation, restoration, regeneration and sanctification there is a condemned sign on your front lawn! Let God Arise in you and his enemies in your life be scattered! Faithful is he who has begun the work in you to complete it!

A personal prophecy that I will share here is that God told me that I would have disappointment in my life on the left side of the comma (,) on the right side of the comma (,) perplexed, but not distressed, persecuted but not forsaken. All you have to do is stay on the right side of the comma and to keep my heart **ONE**!

O is overcoming the natural man through the Spirit of Truth. **N** is having the divine nature of God when we desire a permanent change of wills. God makes a way for us to **E**-extricate ourselves from our natural homeland (self), and move into our inherited promised land! The Shulammite maiden in Songs of Solomon had a dark past and secret sins prior to the seventh chapter of her testimony. But she went in search of the Lover of her soul, and he responded to her right where she was. But there came a time that she had to move outside of her comfort zone to enter the Chamber of the Bride Groom! We will come out as Sarah did calling, Abraham her spouse her Lord! You have Jesus as your Savior, Now Make Him Your Lord!

Satan has nothing in us, except what we have not surrendered and confessed as sin! God's law is sure converting the heart, and he does not have to do anything else, because it has already been done. Everything is set in place for us and we have to possess it, apply it, put it on and work it out in fear and trembling! In Philippians 2:12, Paul says "Wherefore, my beloved, as ye have always obeyed, not a sin my presence only, but now much more in my absence, work out your own salvation with fear and trembling. For it is God which worketh in you both to will and to do his good pleasure. Do all things without murmurings and disputings: That ye may be blameless and harmless, the sons of God, without rebuke, in the midst of a crooked and perverse nation, among whom ye shine as lights in the world; Holding forth the word of life; that I may rejoie in the day of Christ, that I have not run in vain, neither laboured in vain."

The road to oneness is a road that leads to God and it is not crowded and broad with publicans and pharisees, but it is narrow and less traveled. For the purpose of his good pleasure and to have an affect; influence, produce a change, to move or stir an emotional response in the earth towards the heart of God! Once you have a clear understanding of when you were chosen (before the foundation of the world) and that you are his and his banner (meaning a standard has been raised) of love is flying over you and you are accepted and his love is unfailing! Being chosen, allows the one who chose you to have a say in how you live your life! Time for getting to know yourself better, eliminate the hinderances and focus on the prize of the high calling! Bottom line here is where we lose sin consciousness and become righteous conscious! We no longer are sinners and we no longer wear filthy rags and imitation rings! We are clothed in righteousness and have a ring of reconciliation on our finger as sons and daughters of the Father! What will you say then to all these things, are you willing to let go of fears of dependency, intimacy, competition, chaos, victimization, lying, procrastination, chronic avoidance of obligations, sitting in the grey zone, and self-pity.

Stronghold Breaking Prayer

This prayer is adapted from Liberty Savards book "Shattering Your Strongholds" which I highly recommend. Other books recommended you use for this leg of the journey: 1) Pigs in the Parlor and 2)Deliverance for Children and Teens; and the 3)Three Battlegrounds. The enumeration is not order of recommendation, just so that you would see that there are 3 different books.

This is a prayer that I hung on my wall and every morning when I rose and during the day and before I went to bed I would read this prayer out loud for myself and my family **until** I began to see manifestation of the prayer and then God told me that I had asked him in faith, then I should thank him for the answer. The initial prayer may seem as if you are not getting results, but changes will manifest and then you know you have made an impact and you must keep it up until you have gained confidence in your spirit that it is done! Insert "Thank you that" onto each sentence when ready for thanksgiving.

"In the name of Jesus Christ, I bind my body, soul and spirit to the will and purposes of God. I bind myself to the truth of God. I bind myself to an awareness of the power of the blood of Jesus working in my life everyday. I bind my mind to the mind of Christ that I can have the thoughts, purposes and feelings of His heart in me. I bind my feet to the paths you have ordained for me to walk that my steps will be strong and steady. I bind myself to the work of the cross with all of its mercy, truth, love, power, forgiveness and dying to self. I bind myself to God's timing that I may always be on the schedule and in the place that you want me to be. In the name of Jesus Christ, I bind the strong man and I loose his hold on everything he has ever stolen from me. I rebuke his works and loose the power and effects of every deception, device and influence he wants to bring against me. Lord, I repent of having wrong attitudes and thoughts. I renounce them now and ask your forgiveness. I loose every old, wrong pattern of thinking, attitude, idea, desire, belief, habit and behavior that may still be working in me. I tear down, crush, smash and destroy every stronghold I have erected to protect them. I bind myself to the attitudes and patterns of Jesus Christ. I bind myself to the overcoming behavior and spiritual desires that line up with the fruit of the Holy Spirit. Father, I loose any stronghold in my life protecting wrong feelings I have against anyone. Forgive me as I forgive those who have caused me pain, loss or grief. I loose any deisre for retribution and redress In the name of Jesus, I loose the power and the effects of any harsh or hard words or word curses spoken by me, to me or by me. I loose any strongholds connected with them. I loose all generational bondage and their stronghold from myself. Thank you Jesus, that you have promised whatsoever I bind and loose on earth will be bound and loosed in heaven. Amen" Now that we have undressed our soul, we must redress it in the Armor

God has given us through His Righteousness!

Lets' Get Dressed -Ephesians 6

1) Loins Girt with Truth - the girdle held the breastplate in place (guarding the heart) was central to the rest of the armor! The truth makes you uncomfortable when you are not walking in integrity, your intimate areas are covered (secrets) because the

2) Breastplate of Righteousness - protects your heart and enables you to operate in a state of being right before God, because you are submitted to God you are able to resist and he will flee! Because you have done all to stand, so stand!

3) Feet Shod with Preparation of the Gospel of Peace - Roman soldiers shoes wrapped around their ankles with nails on bottom that allowed them to walk with stability, balance and momentum. Do what pleases God and what glorifies him and what keeps your heart at peace.

4) Shield of Faith - First contact with the enemy it is your defense that you meet his attack with and defeat him! Having the word of God in your heart prevents destruction when weapons are formed!

5) Helmet of Salvation - it covers the head so that your mind is on your SALVATION and not your past!

CHAPTER 2

♥

IT IS MY LIFE!

"Satan has nothing in us, except the things we have not repented of and surrendered! These dark things he can work on us with! Because Satan found no shadow or turning in Jesus, he had nothing on Him to defeat Him! God's law is sure and perfect converting the heart! He does not have to do anything else, because it has already been done. Our role is to apply what has been done!

Everything is set. Jesus was driven into the wilderness and came out with victory established for us! The Old Testament Saints could not walk in victory because of what Satan had in them. We are New Testament Saints and we are heirs to the victory Jesus established!

Reference: I Corinthians 2:2 & I Peter 2:21-25

2- It Is My Life!

Conceptionally Influenced!

You now have a choice to wear the filthy rags of unrighteousness or the robe of righteousness because you have a new birth! Knowing that from the moment your parents conceived you and God knitted you in your mothers womb you were set to follow a predestined journey called life. You are not an accident! Scientifically it has been proven that unless there is a chemical compatability between a man and a woman the probability of conception is reduced. Some couples have been married for years and never reproduce. Suddenly, should one of them decide to divorce, and remarry one will either become pregnant or impregnate.[2] Which means some people will never reproduce. So, this journey that you are on by Gods' divine permission before the foundation of the earth is being lived based on the condition of your soul (mind and emotions), spirit and body! Your soul is the place where you experience the war of the flesh! Your spirit is the place where you experience salvation, assurance, security, acceptance and submission to the will of God for your life; according to Romans 12:1. Your body is the place of expression of what is going on internally from the soul and the

---

[2] Source: Fertility research on the Internet on keywords "Chemical Compatibility" and the affect on Conception"

spirit. All of these are influenced by who your parents were intellectually, emotionally, physically and spiritually at the moment in time. I call it a snapshot of history! Because at the exact moment of conception an image was captured of who, what and how you would face the journey called life!

If your father was an alcholic, then an impression was left in your DNA, if your mother was a drug addict it was impressed in your DNA. The Bible says that we are fearfully and wonderfully made! And that we are shapen in iniquity. For this discourse, iniquity is the propensity or the predisposition towards a way of being, doing and experiencing life. It is similar to a photograph being taken at an exact date and time and developed in a dark room that would result in an image of the exact moment and time! You were a snapshot in your mothers womb of who she was and he was at the exact moment and time, and hence came in this world with a set of designer luggage so to speak that you would carry on every leg of your journey! Born with an iniquitous way of looking and living your life. We found ourselves repeating our parents mistakes and behaving as they behaved, laughing and walking as they walked, looking and reacting as they did at that very moment in time. This explanation that I am presenting to you is that without conversion you will spend the rest of your life walking out and in your parents iniquities and having your teeth set on edge from your parents sins! But God has made a way of escape so that your teeth no longer have to be set on edge from their sins. You can work out your soul salvation with fear and trembling before God as he shakes out the things that can not remain so that the things that can remain will remain. He will take out the weaknesses of our iniquities that causes us to walk in the den of iniquity and commit sins against the Word and Will of God as believers. Perhaps your parents are saved today, and they were not saved when you were conceived, and they have spiritual amnesia of how they use to be, or perhaps they have been very forthcoming with you about their weaknesses during your conception. Either way it goes you have a conscious choice to make as a believer to exercise the authority God has given you over the enemy or not! If you are not blind, deaf, mute, or lame and someone else has a certain level of responsibility for your well being then you are the one who must accept responsibility for where you are today! If you are in a good place, praise God! If you are in a chaotic place, look up for your redeemer draws nigh and the day of deliverance is at hand! God does not tempt us, we are tempted by our own desires and lust which were handed down to us from our parents and those we have since developed into our own!

To some of us those iniquities became mountains, valleys,

pits, winding roads, dead ends, crossroads, or condemned dwellings! God says that he will make the high places low and the low places high when we call on him! This is a challenge to you to move outside of the way you were shapened in your mothers womb and move onto the potters' wheel and allow him to remake you again another as he did in Jeremiah 18. God is the same today as he was yesterday and well able to deliver and set your heart free from the baggage of conception and poor choices!

First you must choose this day whom you will serve, if God be God then serve God! End of subject! It is a conscious choice you make to believe that there is a God, and there is no other God beside our God, Elohim! He will shine the light of the word on your darkened iniquites and will reconcile your being with the power of the word, the blood, the name of Jesus and the Holy Spirit. There is a way that seemeth right unto man, but the end thereof is destruction. In Volume 1 we laid a foundation, an understanding of the who, what, where, why and how of the purpose of having a heart of oneness! Now we will address the matters of the heart that obstruct and divide the heart into multiple compartments!

In some individuals this can cause all types of mental, physical and spiritual ailments that are not curable by medical science, but treatable and maintainable with prescriptions! Only

God, Elohim has and will heal, deliver and set free according to our faith! It is already done, we have to bring our level of faith up to the level of word we need to apply. If you can visualize with me a meat or candy thermometer and the temperature that determines if the meat is done at 180 degrees and the thermometer now reads 100, then we know that the meat is not fully cooked. When the required temperature of 180 is reached inside the meat we have a fully cooked piece of meat. Let's apply this to our faith and the word of God! The word of God says that the just shall live by faith! When God told Abraham to look as far as "his" eyes could see, and that would be the land that he would give him. Just think God was asking Abraham to stretch his eyesight to its capacity, and he looked through the eyes of faith and God gave him what he could observe. But this was before the Holy Spirit was poured out! Today, God says look as far as you can see and trust me for what you can not see and I will give you exceedingly and abundantly above what you may ask or imagine!

When faith rises to the level of power and expectancy that exist in that rhema Word of God we have combustion, ignition if you would, as a lit match when it strikes against the side of the matchbox. I hear the sound of ignition in the spirit, just like I hear the sound of the match igniting when struck against that box. It is the "Power of Agreement" that we experience, when our faith meets the faith of Gods' Word we walk in agreement. This is when faith becomes unshakeable, it is what becomes known to us and no one can move you off of what you now believe because it has become alive inside of your spirit!

This is a quickening that makes us leap and rejoice, run and shout and scream as if something is overloading our emotions! It is, because it is the realm of the supernatural that we have entered! This volume is meant to take the Word of God and create that dunamis force that will explode and extricate and manifest the diamonds in your coal mine! We must come forth as pure gold, loving the Lord our God with our whole hearts on a road that is narrow! This narrow road is the journey to oneness! Many seek after and few press their way into victory! Join me won't you!

The roads are figurative of directional paths that are crowded with the people who are like the publicans in the Bible. Lets label them "public access" roads, then there are roads we will label as "refuge for the soul" that lead to cities of refuge - where God avenges us, like the man injured on the side of the road to Damascus, then there are roads of righteousness we will call "private access" that lead us to the face and house of God. This private access road is narrow and infrequently traveled by many, because it requires strict adherence to the voice of God, and following the word as it becomes a light unto your pathway, the road is filled with pebbles and stones. In the old testament travelers wore lanterns around their ankles that would grant them light for their feet to determine if the ground they were walking on was safe. This is what the Word of God does for us on this narrow and private road, it leads to holiness, while the roads that lead to sin are broad and filled with people on the journey of life. Has your journey been filled with peril and chaos? Can you conclusively say that you have no need of a light for your feet to walk by? Will you play your life by chance or by divine appointment?

Assume the Position

What do you do after you have decided to assume the position of a heart after God? Assuming the position is found in the passage of scripture Ephesians 6:13-14 that says after having done all to to stand, STAND!

Dissecting the word heart H | EAR | T -

Use the ear of your heart to listen to the voice of God; in simpler terms practice the art of listening in the spirit with the ear of your heart. Within the word heart you can also find (hear, ear and art). The heart is the tool by which we practice this art form.

In I Samuel 20:2 - we see the phrase "uncover my ear" which means to reveal. In Isaiah 6:10, and Jeremiah 6:10 - the phrase "ears dull" or "closed" or "uncircumcised" denotes one who is inattentive and disobedient. When God is spoken of as hearing the prayers of his people in Psalms 34:15, we see "His ears are open to their cry."

As believers we hear the voice of God through the communion of the Holy Spirit. He leads and guides us into all truth, because he is the prophet on board revealing the will of the Prophet to us as we listen for instruction and revelation as we take the journey through the fellowship of his suffering. Our journey carries us through the paths of separation, accusation, persecution, crucifixion, burial, resurrection, redemption, reconciliation and ascencion.

Your Journey

Do you still want to hold the opinion that your life is your own? Just in case your answer is yes; how are you doing so far? Have you attained what you consider success in your life without Gods' help? "What know ye not that your body is the temple of the Holy Ghost which is in you, which ye have of God, and ye are not your own?

For ye are bought with a price: therefore glorify God in your body, and in your spirit, which are Gods'. (I Corinthians

6:19-20)

You have a wonderful job, money in the bank, a spouse, two children, a vested retirement fund, cars, social status, and all the things you could ever imagine having! Bravo! When you are sitting down in that comfy chair for two or lying down in the bed next to your wonderful spouse do you feel as if you are the only one there? Yes, physically their hands are touching you, and you them. Yet, something inside of you feels the need to repeat the act of intercourse as many times as physically possible, make a midnight run on the fridge, get up and stare out the window and look at the trees or the birds.

You can't quite put your finger on what is going on inside of you. Your spouse draws near and notices the blank stare in your face, and he or she inquires if you are okay. You respond yes, but there is an echo that you hear inside of you when you said that and it sounds like a house without any furnishings. You ponder what is wrong? You begin to enumerate all of the things and reasons you have to be happy and why you should be dancing on the ceiling!

Yet, there is a tinge of something that does not seem to be right inside of you. You know your life, the thing that you have mastered all by your wonderful self. You are so proud, because you have proven that the amercican dream can be accomplished with a lot of hard work and sacrifice, you have paid your dues and it's time to enjoy the rewards.

What is this then that you can not quite put your hand on! It is right t-h-e-re, and you can almost touch it, explain it, yet it is elusive and undescribable and you can't quite make it out. It's kind of dark around the space and you think if I could only get some understanding, or talk to someone who could help me understand what I am feeling! Perhaps a flashlight, candle or something to get a better look I would know what it is! It is an annoying sensation like having a piece of food stuck in between your teeth! You might floss, brush or pick at it with your nails and it just won't budge! Sometimes, it takes longer than we would like to get the food dislodged, and giving it some alone time seems to help! **Alone** to do what? Well, your mouth acids begin to break it down, a couple of sips of water or the next bite of food you eat. Even after you remove the lodged food from your teeth you are left with this phantom feeeling that it is still stuck in between your teeth. Yet, you glance in the mirror to see if it is still there, even though you know it is gone. One of the many things we all have in common, no matter who we are is time! Inside the spirit we experience such moments that things seem amiss, and a sense that time has passed you by! Have I really achieved what I wanted to out of my life, am I truly happy and can I honestly say that my journey is completed and this is how history will remember me! Or is this gnawing feeling inside of you a call to a greater destination to go beyond where I am to finding out what my purpose is in the world! As you journey through life there is a reality that there are two opposing forces! Good and Evil! A Problem and a Solution! Are you a problem or a solution? Are you Good or Evil? God rains on the just and the unjust! Time out for good behavior, does not exist in the kingdom of God!

Time!

Yes, time! We all have been given a measure of time in the earth to complete our assigned journey! Do you know what your purpose is? What your assignment is? I use to wonder the same thing myself! Until I had a conversation with a very wise old man, who had lived his life to the fullest!

This is what he had to say to me, "There IS an evil which I have seen under the sun, and it is common among men: A man to whom God hath given riches, wealth, and honour, so that he wanteth nothing for his soul of all that he desireth, yet God giveth him not power to eat thereof, but a stranger eateth it: this is vanity, and it is an evil disease.

If a man beget an hundred children, and live many years, so that the days of his years be many, and his soul be not filled with good, and also that he have no burial; I say, that an untimely birth is better than he. For he cometh in with vanity, and departeth in darkness, and his name shall be covered with darkness.

Moreover he hath not seen the sun, nor known any thing: this hath more rest than the other." And then he said, "A GOOD name is better than precious ointment; and the day of death than the day of one's birth."

He went on and said, "Consider the work of God: for who can make that straight, which he hath made crooked."

Then he said, "Also take no heed unto all words that are spoken; lest thou hear thy servant curse thee: For oftentimes also thine own heart knoweth that thou thyself likewise hast cursed others…That which is far off, and exceeding deep, who can find it out?…Whoso keepeth the commandment shall feel no evil thing: and a wise man's heart discerneth both **time and judgment**. Because to **every purpose there is time and judgment**, therefore the misery of man is great upon him."

Then he indicated to me that I should make the best of my life by saying that, "FOR ALL this is considered in my heart even to declare all this, that the righteous, and the wise, and their works, are in the hand of God: no man knoweth either love or hatred by all that is before them. All things come alike to them all:…Whatsoever thy hand findeth to do, do it with thy might; for there is nor work, nor device, nor knowledge, nor wisdom in the grave, whither thou goest.

I returned, and saw under the sun, that the race is not to the swift, nor the battle to the strong, neither yet bread to the wise, nor yet riches to men of understanding, nor yet favour to men of skill; **but time and chance** happeneth to them all…A wise man's heart is at his right hand; but a fool's heart at his left…As thou knowest not what is the way of the spirit, nor how the bones do grow in the womb of her that is with child: even so thou knowest not the works of God who maketh all…Rejoice, O young man, in thy youth; and let thy heart cheer thee in the days of thy youth, and walk in the ways of thine heart, and in the sight of thine eyes: but know thou, that for all these things God will bring thee into judgment.

Therefore remove sorrow from thy heart, and put away evil from thy flesh: for childhood and youth are vanity." He concluded by saying, "REMEMBER NOW thy Creator in the days of thy youth, while the evil days come not, nor the years draw nigh, when thou shalt say, I have no pleasure in them;…because man goeth to his long home, and the mourners go about the streets…then shall the dust return to the earth as it was: and the spirit shall return unto God who gave it…Let us hear the conclusion of the whole matter: **Fear God, and keep his commandments: for this is the whole duty of man.** For God shall bring every work into judgment, with every secret thing, whether it be good, or whether it be evil."

This man as you can tell was Solomon, and these are the words spoken within Chapters 6 through Chapter 12 of Ecclesiastes. His most prolific statement to me was, "TO EVERY thing there is a season, and a time to every purpose under the sun." Chapter 3 of Ecclesiates.

Now Again I reiterate that what every man has in common in the world is TIME!

Time to live as you choose to live, and die as you choose to die! We can not serve ourselves and God. And this is what was found in the writings of David, "TRULY GOD is good to Israel, even to such as are of a clean heart. But as for me, my feet were almost gone; my steps had well nigh slipped. For I was envious at the foolish, when I saw the prosperity of the wicked…Whom have I in heaven but thee? My flesh and my heart faileth: but God is the strength of my heart, and my portion for ever.

For, lo, they that are far from thee shall perish: thou hast destroyed all them that go a-whoring from thee. But it is good for me to draw near to God: I have put my trust in the Lord God, that I may declare all thy works." Solomon and David found the answer in the face and presence of God as he showed them that there is a way that seemeth right unto man but the end there of is destruction! This is not the end of the matter as long as you are above ground, God has given us…

A Way of Escape

Nine-fold

God has provided a way out of the old ways of being! Before Christ we walked continually in a **nine-fold** state of sin: 1) a vain mind, 2) a darkened understanding, 3) alienated from God, 4) ignorant of God, 5) blind in our hearts, 6) feelings of inadequacy, 7) lustful, 8) unclean 9) and greedy.

Four-fold

We were governed by the **four** spirits of rebellion which are the 1) principalities, 2) authorities, 3) world rulers and 4) spiritual wickedness. **Scripture Reference:** Ephesians 6:12, Colossians 2:10, Colossians 1:16-18.

Seven-fold

We have been given the **seven-fold** blessings that lead to perfection found in Ephesians 4:14. To 1) become mature, 2) established in the faith, 3) rooted and grounded in truth, 4) freedom from deception, 5) speak the truth in love, 6) constant spiritual growth, 7) harmony with all others in Christs.

Eighteen-fold

From this place of transition on our journey we gain access to **the eighteen-fold** life of a believer. Which are to 1) learn of Christ, 2) hearers and doers of the word, 3) putting off the old man, 4) renewal in our mind, 5) putting on the new man, 6) put away lying and speak truthfully, 7) being angry without sin, 8) resisting the devil, 9) quit stealing, 10) work for a living, 11) give to the poor, 12) use the tongue right, 13) grieve not the Holy Spirit, 14) put away bitterness, wrath, clamour, evil speaking and malice, 15) be kind, tender-hearted, forgiving, 16) followers of God, 17) walk in love, 18) removal of fornication, homosexuality, covetousness, filthiness, foolish talking, sexual indiscretions and jesting.

Scriptural reference: Ephesians 4:20, Romans 1:18, Colossians 3:5-10.

Let us put away childishness and move onto the....

Pursuit of Gods' Divine Success

Seven-fold Oneness

That is to take this journey with the intent of entering into the seven-fold oneness of God so that we may become as 1) one body (the Church), 2) one spirit (the Holy Spirit), 3) one hope (the Christian Calling), experiencing 4) one Lord (Jesus Christ), 5) one faith (the gospel), 6) one baptism (into the body of Christ), 7) and one God (Father of us all).

Reference Scriptures: Ephesians 4:4-6, I Corinthians 12:13, Galatians 3:27.

We are closing down the time that we spend divided between the path of the righteous and the path of the wicked! Spending time on both roads seeking the pursuit of success is draining and conflicted! We who are righteous are compelled to do the following, and that is to observe that; "This book of the law shall not depart out of thy mouth; but thou shalt meditate therein day and night, that thou mayest observe to do according to all that is written therein: for then thou shalt make thy way prosperous, and then thou shalt have good success." We are to be strong in the Lord, be strong in his power, put on the whole armour, stand, loins girted with truth, feet shod with the preparation of the gospel of peace, the shield of faith, the helmet of salvation, the sword of the spirit, pray in the spirit, watch in prayer, acquire strength and to increase in strength. When we do this we have these blessings bestowed on us: The ability to stand against the enemy, ability to withstand all attacks and ability to quench every fiery dart of Satan! **Scripture Reference: Ephesians 6.**

The wicked are not so!

According to Jeremiah 29:11 and 3 John, God plans for us to be successful with godliness and contentment.

In Jeremiah 29:11-13, God says "For I know the thoughts that I think toward you, saith the Lord, thoughts of peace, and not of evil, to give you an expected end...

Then shall ye call upon me, and ye shall go and pray unto me, and I will hearken unto you. And ye shall seek me, and find me, when ye shall search for me with **all** your heart. And I will be found of you, saith the Lord: and I will turn away your capitivity, and I will gather you from all the nations, and from all the places whither I have driven you, saith the Lord; and I will bring you again into the place **whence I caused you to be carried away captive.**

Because ye have said, The Lord hath raised us up prophets in Babylon;"

And in 3 John 2, "Beloved, I wish **above all things** that thou mayest prosper and be in health, even as thy soul prospereth."

God's way of bringing us into success is a balanced way of living as he has ordained for us to live! He is not an extremist or out of balance! As his children when we take **our journey** we are to mark him and walk becoming of his name in the earth.

Journeying onto the road of oneness, is a step of faith in time, to the measure of time that God has given to us upon the earth.

It is the kiros of God, never late but always on time on the road toward walking in oneness of heart and faith.

It is hard to group along the lines of Christianity today because we are mingled into denominations that believe not that Jesus is the son of God! Growing up you would hear the jesting and jeering of Christians as those old "Holy Rollers" when you said you were a christian. Today this word "Christianity" has taken on a very different life over the last few decades. It seems to be more of a label, a marketing tool, a fad and a movement in the mind of the public. Yet God says, let the wheat grow with the tare! For this reason we must know one another after the spirit, so that as we encounter true believers who are on the assignment of manifesting in the earth the believers authority we will recognize each other. Our life should be so obvious that the Bible says we are to be living epistles, easily ready of men, according to II Corinthians 3:2!

Because we have been delivered from the accursed things such as the reproach of men, shame, bitterness, barrenesss, deception, rejection, abandonment, poverty and everything that would exalt itself against the authority of the word, the name, the blood and the spirit of God placed upon us from the point of conception through the redeeming power of what Christ has accomplished. The only wise God our Saviour has made a way of escape and it is through the door; Jesus Christ. Walk this way, and let him order our steps and lead us out of the wilderness. We want the shape of God in our hearts, S.H.A.P.E. defined, what is your Spiritual Gift, Heart (Passion), Abilities (developed gift), Personality (Attitude driven), Experiences (those that have shaped you) because we are the sum total of our experiences great and small.

Reading of the Wills

A.W.Tozer, states that "Anyone who might feel reluctant to surrender his will to the will of another should remember Jesus' words, `*Whosoever committeth sin is the servant of sin.*' We must of necessity be servant to someone, either to God or to sin. The sinner prides himself on his independence, completely overlooking the fact that he is the weak slave of the sins that rule his members…

…The man who surrenders to Christ exchanges a cruel slave driver for a kind and gentle Master whose yoke is easy and whose burden is light.

...Made as we were in the image of God we scarcely find it strange to take again our God as our All. God was our original habitat and our hearts cannot but feel at home when they enter again that ancient and beautiful abode. I hope it is clear that there is a logic behind God's claim to pre-eminence. That place is His by every right in earth or heaven. While we take to ourselves the place that is His the whole course of our lives is out of joint. Nothing will or can restore order till our hearts make the great decision: God shall be exalted above.

...`*Them that honour me I will honour,*' said God once to a priest of Israel, and that ancient law of the Kingdom stands today unchanged by the passing of time or the changes of dispensation. The whole Bible and every page of history proclaim the perpetuation of that law. `*If any man serve me, him will my Father honour,*' said our Lord Jesus, tying in the old with the new and revealing the essential unity of His ways with men. Sometimes the best way to see a thing is to look at its opposite. Eli and his sons are placed in the priesthood with the stipulation that they honor God in their lives and ministrations.

...This they fail to do, and God sends Samuel to announce the consequences. Unknown to Eli this law of reciprocal honor has been all the while secretly working, and now the time has come for judgment to fall. Hophni and Phineas, the degenerate priests, fall in battle, the wife of Hophni dies in childbirth, Israel flees before her enemies, the ark of God is captured by the Philistines and the old man Eli falls backward and dies of a broken neck. Thus stark tragedy followed upon Eli's failure to honor God.

...Now set over against this almost any Bible character who honestly tried to glorify God in his earthly walk. See how God winked at weaknesses and overlooked failures as He poured upon His servants grace and blessing untold. Let it be Abraham, Jacob, David, Daniel, Elijah or whom you will; honor followed honor as harvest the seed. The man of God set his heart to exalt God above all; God accepted his intention as fact and acted accordingly. Not perfection, but holy intention made the difference.

...In our Lord Jesus Christ this law was seen in simple perfection. In His lowly manhood He humbled Himself and gladly gave all glory to His Father in heaven. He sought not His own honor, but the honor of God who sent Him. `*If I honour myself,*' He said on one occasion, `*my honour is nothing; it is my Father that honoureth me.*' (John 8:54) So far had the proud Pharisees departed from this law that they could not understand one who honored God at his own expense. `*I honour my Father,*' said Jesus to them, `*and ye do dishonour me.*'

...Another saying of Jesus, and a most disturbing one, was put in the form of a question, '*How can ye believe, which receive honour one of another, and seek not the honour that cometh from God alone?*' (John 5:44) If I understand this correctly Christ taught here the alarming doctrine that the desire for honor among men made belief impossible. Is this sin at the root of religious unbelief? Could it be that those 'intellectual difficulties' which men blame for their inability to believe are but smoke screens to conceal the real cause that lies behind them? Was it this greedy desire for honor from man that made men into Pharisees and Pharisees into Deicides? Is this the secret back of religious self-righteousness and empty worship? I believe it may be. Who will make the once-for-all decision to exalt Him over all? Such are these precious to God above all treasures of earth or sea. In them God finds a theater where He can display His exceeding kindness toward us in Christ Jesus. With them God can walk unhindered, toward them He can act like the God He is.

...In speaking thus I have one fear; it is that I may convince the mind before God can win the heart. For this God-above-all position is one not easy to take. The mind may approve it while not having the consent of the will to put it into effect. While the imagination races ahead to honor God, the will may lag behind and the man never guess how divided his heart is. The whole man must make the decision before the heart can know any real satisfaction. God wants us all, and He will not rest till He gets us all. No part of the man will do.

...Let us pray over this in detail, throwing ourselves at God's feet and meaning everything we say. No one who prays thus in sincerity need wait long for tokens of divine acceptance. God will unveil His glory before His servant's eyes, and He will place all His treasures at the disposal of such a one, for He knows that His honor is safe in such consecrated hands. *O God, be thou exalted over my possessions. Nothing of earth's treasures shall seem dear unto me if only Thou art glorified in my life. Be Thou exalted over my friendships. I am determined that Thou shalt be above all, though I must stand deserted and alone in the midst of the earth. Be Thou exalted above my comforts. Though it mean the loss of bodily comforts and the carrying of heavy crosses I shall keep my vow made this day before Thee. Be Thou exalted over my reputation. Make me ambitious to please Thee even if as a result I must sink into obscurity and my name be forgotten as a dream. Rise, O Lord, into Thy proper place of honor, above my ambitions, above my likes and dislikes, above my family, my health and even my life itself. Let me decrease that Thou mayest increase, let me sink that Thou mayest rise above. Ride forth upon me as Thou didst ride into Jerusalem mounted upon the humble little beast, a colt, the foal of an ass, and let me hear the children cry to Thee, `Hosanna in the highest'."* We are encouraged to take the journey and follow after Jesus Christ!

In the Footsteps of Jesus

Reference Scripture: Acts 9:1-8

A brief narrative of the meaning of the names of some of the cities on Jesus' journey help us to understand the travail and suffering of his short time on this earth to do the will of his Father God:

<u>Nazareth</u>; Seen as a Germ, <u>Bethany</u>; House of Depression or Misery (Mark 11 - 15), <u>Jerusalem</u>; dwelling of peace (Mark 1:1-15a, Mark 16:1-2, Mark 9:20, <u>Galilee</u>; (ring or circle), <u>Capernaum</u>; (village of Nahum)(comfort)), <u>Bethpage</u>; (house of unripe figs), <u>Mount of Olives</u>; (orchard of anointing), <u>Joseph of Arimathea;</u> (may God add heights), <u>Gethesemane</u>; (pressing place of the anointing), <u>Pontius</u>; (belonging to) Pilate; (one armed with a dart). These places are indicative of the journey we all travel and because he was victorious he has left a path for us to be victorious overcomers and not failing as Adam. When we examine these places by name meaning we see nothing but Jesus ministering along the way in the midst of rejection, misery, pressings and determination to finish the course laid before him. When Jesus needed refreshing and restoration he expected to find it on the way in the things God had created. He expected the created things to be fulfilling the purpose for which

they were created.

Because the fig indicates medicinal healing II Kings 20:7 appearing at the beginning of summer and spring. These are the most productive periods for harvesting figs. Failure to bear fruit was seen as a great calamity. Song 2:13, Luke 21:29-30, most of them drop off the tree before perfected. In the winter they are unripe and the fig grows under the leaves and do not ripen at the normal season but hang upon the trees during the winter, can be found wild, but mainly cultivated in Palestine since ancient times. When the leaves appear an there is no fruit on the tree, it will be barren for that season - Matthew 21:19-22.

Jesus curses the fig tree about the beginning of April the figs had ample time to ripen.

Scripturally it produces rich sweet fruit (Judges 9:11), and is not found in desert places, abound in Egypt and Canaan, Often grew wild, sometimes planted in vineyards, progated by Jesus, required cultivation, fruit formed after winter, leaves put forth as a sign of summer approaching, reasonable for Jesus to expect fruit that could be eaten fresh from the tree or to have cakes made, to be gathered, first ripened esteemed as used in miraculous healing of Hezekiah, sold in market place and sent as presents. So why did Jesus curse the fig tree? Because it stood in the presence of God denying the power of God that was locked within it to produce the required fruit at the required season. When Jesus approaches us after salvations has been received he expects to find us productive and able to provide healing to those who come our way. Yet, some believers ask in the midst of service the question whats' my motivation and what is in this for me? They live the journey of salvation with mediocrity and doing just enough to get by, lukewarm and carnal minded. Not seeking to fulfill Gods' expectations that we should manifest as the Sons of God in the earth!

    The fig tree has the audacity to stand in the presence of Jesus and not manifest! The Bible says in Proverbs 26:2 that a curse undeserved will not be effective. The fig tree did not merit absolution in my own thoughts because it is like the day of judgment when God will ask us to give account of ourselves there will be no mercy! We as believers come together and say we are standing on Holy Ground, but don't have the manifestation. We look, walk and talk like Christians, but we don't have the signs and wonders as we are capable of having to their fullness. We have passed from death to life as the ransomed and redeemed. We became the sons of God, when Jesus was sown into the earth as seed. Seed bears after its kind, after Jesus became the first begotten of the dead standing at the mouth of the grave and calling out to us Lazarus' come forth if you would!

O death where is your sting, and o grave where is our victory!

We must believe that we have received this power to raise the dead, so that we can speak to the dead issues in our lives, and prophecy like Ezekiel to the dry bones and command them to live. If we shall not then who shall! We are none of his, we are anathema, against him! He gave us life from the grave so that we could walk in the power of the resurrection (His spirit being poured out upon all dead and stinking flesh). The water of the word resurrects the dead and the deadness just like adding water to an easter lilly that appears to be at the brink of death or already dead, just a few ounces of water and it comes back strong. We are to desire him for the purpose of Him finding us in the unity of the faith, One Purpose, One Faith and One Sound!

Seeking His Face

Face metaphorically means to be in the sight or in the mind and will and purpose of someone. Luke 1:35-37, Acts 8:17-25

How is the fig tree like the unfruitful believer standing in the face of God himself? It looks like a tree planted for the purpose of bearing fruit, a specific fruit type (fig). Fitting in with the scenery of the land and the time trying to pass. But the smell of the tree gives it away, and causes others to see that it is not acting like a fig tree. Meaning it must not believe it is a fig tree, it has not fruit; but having the form of a fig tree akin to having a form of godliness but denying the power thereof.

We have asked God, why, how long and when will our prayers be answered. When is it going to be my turn? God has the answer, he knows you are already on Satans' hit list, and in order to escape we must let go of what lies behind us, leaving our natural home and make the decision to cross over the Red Sea and Jordan River into the promised land. The Red Sea, swallowed up death, hell and the grave that was in pursuit of our souls. The Jordan River represents our place of decision. Will you decide to follow Gods plan for your life and begin the journey of salvation as the Shulammite maiden did?

When she chose to surrender all, her companions began noticing and commenting on the attractiveness of her person, and God looked upon her, even though she had a testimony of a dark past and secret sins. She went in search of the face of God, and he responded to her right where she was. But then there came a time that she was required to meet him outside of her comfort zone and enter into the Chamber of the Bride Groom! We will come out as Sarah did, calling Abraham Lord! When she responded to God, this is what he had to say to her in the Song of Solomon, chapter 7. "How beautiful are thy feet with shoes, O prince's daughter! the joints of thy thighs are like jewels, the work of thy hands of a cunning workman. Thy navel is like a round goblet, which wanteth not liquor; thy belly is like an heap of wheat set about with lillies. They two breasts are like two young roes that are twins. Thy neck is as a tower of ivory; thine eyes like the fish-pools in Hesh-bon, by the gate of Bath-rabbim, thy nose is as the tower of Lebanon, which looketh toward Damascus. Thine head upon thee is like Carmel, and the hair of thine head like purple; the king is held in the galleries. How fair and how pleasant art thou, O love, for delights! This thy stature is like to a palm tree, and thy breasts shall be as clusters of the vine, and the smell of thy nose like apples; And the roof of thy mouth like the best wine for my beloved, that goeth down sweetly, causing the lips of those that are asleep to speak. I am my beloved's and his desire is toward me. Come, my beloved, let us go forth into the field; let us lodge in the villages. Let us get up early to the vineyards; let us see if the vine flourish, whether the tender grape appear, and the pomegranates bud forth; there will I give thee my loves. The mandrakes give a smell, and at our gates are all manner of pleasant fruits, new and old, which I have laid up for thee, O my beloved."

We are not to be of those who draw back, but like those who believed before us. (Psalms 5:1-10 and Psalms 19:8-14)

The denial of the power of God and the doubt that we will be held accountable produces in us barreness. This fig tree was alongside the road, and the custom was to let strangers that passed by eat and be refreshed from the fruit. This tree required cultivation and for this reason God did not place it in the wilderness (desert) but in a lush place of green pastures with the expectation of a return on his investment. The fig tree in Jeremiah 29:17 were a species producing vile and worthless fruit, but in Genesis 3:7-9, leaves were used by Adam for covering, and in John 1:48-50, afforded a thick shade, Luke 3:7-9, they were often unfruitful, the enemies devoured them and eaten by locust.

Illustration

Like mere professors of religion and sitting under one's own prosperity and peace. Matthew 7:16-20.

Application

Good saints (fruit of good works), of wicked men. First ripe of the father of the jewish faith (Church). Untimely and dropping of the wicked ripe with judgment (Nahum 3:12) Amorites Amos 2:9-16, fruit above and roots below. Roots seen as the parents and the fruit the children.

Revelation

The fig tree had the audacity to stand in the presence of Jesus and not have the sign expected in the expected season! A curse undeserved will not produce, Proverbs 26:2.

We as believers come together and say we are standing on Holy ground, but don't have the sign that is expected in the season. We stand and look and smell as if we are believers but if we do not believe that Christ has risen from the dead -- then we are none of his. To a christian believer we have had to pass through death to receive his life in us. If we are afraid of seeing the dead risen, then we are none of his, nor should we confess salvation! Salvation is redemption from death, hell and the grave! The first begotten of the dead who stood at the mouth of the grave in the cemetery of a borrowed tomb from a distant relative and commanded the dead in righteousness imputed to get up and the saints of old could not stay in the grave, but were seen walking through the city. The message in his mouth was "o death where is your sting, and o grave where is your victory."

We must believe that we have received this power to raise the dead, so that we can speak to the dead issues in our lives, and prophecy like Ezekiel to the dry bones and command them to live. If we shall not then who shall! We are none of his, we are anathema, against him! He gave us life from the grave so that we could walk in the power of the resurrection (His spirit being poured out upon all dead and stinking flesh). The water of the word resurrects the dead and the deadness just like adding water to an easter lilly that appears to be at the brink of death or already dead, just a few ounces of water and it comes back strong.

CHAPTER 3

♥

CHRISTIAN

*We have just enough religion to make us hate,
but not enough to make us love one another.*
—Jonathan Swift

3- Christian: Walk This Way

Neither wast thou washed...[nor] salted...nor swaddled." Ezekiel 16:4

How come only one in ten people who make a commitment to Christ, are still serving Him 5 years later? Ezekiel gives us some answers:

(1) You must be washed! Your spiritual protection against dirt, disease, and death is "the washing of water by the Word" (Ephesians 5:26 and John 15:3).

(2) You must be salted! In Hebrew culture, they rubbed salt on newborn babies to toughen their skins so that they could be handled without bruising. Too many of us need "special handling." We're touchy. If we're corrected, we get defensive. Only when you've been "salted" by mature love and non-legalistic acceptance, can you be really open and honest.

(3) You must be swaddled! When we're first born into God's family, we're vulnerable. We need to be covered and protected. That's the value of Christian fellowship; it wraps you up tightly in the arms of love and says, "You don't ever have to go back to the old life again! You can begin afresh. You can be healed of your painful past. You can have good times and good relationships instead of bad ones." Have you been washed, salted, and swaddled?" (Bob Gass, Word for the Day)

What hinders us from the success God has predestined us for? Is it our own deceitful hearts and motivations? Is it how we define success within the ranks of chrisianity that cause us great dismay? We have taken a chapter from the worlds' system and wrapped it in scripture.

We have become people who wear and apply the label of christianity within the church, without the life of christianity in our hearts. It is a painful thing now to see the statistics that say divorce is highest ever in the christian community. We are truly in the dispensation of the wheat growing with the tare. "The body becomes stronger as its' members become healthier. The whole church of God gains when the members that compose it begin to seek a better and higher life." A.W. Tozer

There are many who say they are christians with their lips and they take surveys and fill out forms as christians when asked to weigh in on this subjects, but are as sounding brass and tinkling cymbals, having a form of godliness but denying the power thereof!

We see "christians" who are practicing homosexuality in the pulpit and the pews, who are eastern philosophers who claim that christianity is a part of their religious program among many other religions they practice. If it was not okay by God during the time of Sodom and Gomorrah, then why is it okay today? God is the same yesterday, today and forevermore! He changes not, so who decided that "christians" can do as they please and reinvent the Word of God? How are we saved, is it by faith? In Psalms 34:5 it says that "They looked unto him, and were lightened: and their faces were not ashamed." Distractions may hinder us, but…after each brief excursion away from Him the attention will return again and rest upon Him like a wandering bird coming back to its window." A.W. Tozer

When will the true believers and the true followers of Christ really stand and be accounted for? On the day of judgment! Yes, but in the meantime a standard has to be raised within the walls of the church and the world that becomes a highway in the wilderness for men who are stumbling in the dark to see the true light of Jesus Christ! We are children of the light and the salt of the earth, to shine in the darkness and to preserve the ways of holiness to a lost and dying world! On this journey towards oneness with Heaven, as Jesus is one with God; we will confront ourselves at the y-intersection of the path of righteousness and the path of unrighteousness. Stop straddling the lanes, and fence sitting.

It is by faith that we look upward into the author and finisher of our faiths face. "…and it shall come to pass, that everyone that is bitten, when he looketh upon it, shall live…and it came to pass, that if a serpent had bitten an man, when he beheld the serpent of brass, he lived." Numbers 21:4-9 and this passage points to Jesus in the New Testament in John 3:14-15, where it says that Moses lifted up the serpent in the wilderness, ever so must the son of man be lifted up! That whosoever believeth in him should not perish, but have eternal life." We examine as reference the Old Testament and into the New Testament with the internal eye of the believing heart.

Jesus when he looked at his Father, did so with belief that he was able to complete that which he had begun in him. Looking up into heaven, he blessed, and brake, and gave bread to this disciples. (Matthew 14:19) Jesus' power laid in his looking without distraction at his Father according to John 5:19-21. Faith redirects our sight away from sin and its selfish agenda. Unbelief places self on the throne and propels us to walk before God as Satan did with his "I will be lifted up attitude". Faith does not regard self, it is preoccupied with God. What would seek to hinder us passes away from us and we obtain a true perspective and perception of the hindrances to our faith walk, our journey to oneness.

What keeps us from walking on the road to oneness can be found in what ails us. Ordinarily, I might consider spending an enormous amount of time developing this subject on my own. But God is telling me to be brief and to the point, so here goes. What's ailing us is either a love or a hate thing! We either love too much or hate something or someone! Simply, put we are out of balance. There is a thin line that exist they say between love and _ _ _ _! You fill in the blank. And to some level this is true! God says how can we love him, if we hate our brother whom we see everyday....when we have not even seen him! The love of God - Agape is not in us! We bite and devour one another wihin the body and think nothing of it! We form groups, cliques, schisms, and other isms within the walls of the church and shout all around one another, and pretend that the love of God is in our heart! It is a stinch in the nostrils of God, yet let the wheat grow with the tare, until we all come into the unity of the faith!. There is only one God, one Lord, one Faith and one Baptism! We must all follow the same road to achieve oneness that will lead us into the unit of the faith! And that road is narrow and less crowded. When can we say that we have achieved the oneness of heart? These are areas that I want to review with you as stumbling blocks and roots of bitterness that will definitely choke out the love of God and present strife and disharmony within your own heart! I have been instructed by God to examine hatred, abuse and post-traumatic stress as obstacles to wholeness and unity! Let us walk right this way!

This is the Way

Jeremiah 29:12, "Then shall you call upon me, and ye shall go and pray unto me, and I will hearken unto you."

Through the many broken issues of your life, God is speaking to your heart. But how can you hear him, if your heart is broken, and divided in may separate pieces, and the noises won't stop. The Bible states that a…"house divided against itself cannot stand." And this is what we are, are houses, triune beings. In need of restoration from the damages of sin, until we apply the restoring power of God we are sub-standard dwellings. Let God the Master Carpenter arise in you and (your)/his enemies be scattered!

You may be wondering what could I have possibly gone through in my life that qualifies me to say this to anyone! I went in search of whom my soul loveth and found him! I stopped wandering the dark places looking for comfort and raced to the altar of my heart and became His love. I will share a dream with you that I had. In this dream I was running from building to building on this street looking for someone, I believe it was love that I was searching for, and then finally on this same street I entered into a building and it was the church were I was attending at the time, and I rushed into the sanctuary, because I had a sense of what I was looking for was in there. As I entered I noticed a gentlemen dressed in a tuxedo standing at the altar with his arms outstretched towards me, He said to me I have been waiting for you all this time! This was not a natural man, because I sensed the presence of God all around and that was when God revealed to me that I had finally gotten my act together! He became my beloved, my betrothed, my husband and my love! He told me that He had from that point on placed a banner over me and that banner was his love for me! (Song of Solomon 2:4)

Totally and unconditionally He was mine, and I was His!

What Satan meant for evil in my life, God has turned around and told Satan the party is over and drew a blood line and dared him to go any further! He raised an ensign, a standard at the place where I met Him at the altar of my heart and spoke this word "He who began a good work in me will carry it onto completion" (Philippians 1:6)

Out of a perfect mess of living lies, tangled relationships, the Spirit of the Lord raised up a standard and told the adversary - ENOUGH! Again another word He spoke to me was found in Jeremiah 18:4, it was marred so He made IT again another vessel. He began a work of restoration and rebirthing in me that created a place to bring forth the LIVING TRUTH of the Word of God in me.

The ties that had bound and entangled me were broken, and were burned to ashes and placed under the soles of my feet. God surrounded and filled me with HIS Coventant of adoption and also became my ABBA, Daddy! His last Will and Testament that gave me power to love Him with my whole heart, soul, mind and body.

Come Away With Me

Jeremiah 29:13 "And ye shall seek me, and find me, when ye shall search for me with all your heart."

In 1989, the spirit of the Lord directed me to draw closer to Him, and he would draw closer to me. For three morning straight at 3 a.m., I was awaken to write down the revelation for my life. Not fully understanding the purpose God had for me as I wrote. I simply obeyed! Two years later God began to call that revelation forth from within me, and began to unfold the revelation further, and confirmed the revelation with a second scripture found in I Thessalonians 5:23-24, "And the very God of peace sanctify you <u>wholly</u>; and I pray God your whole spirt and soul and body be preserved blameless unto the coming of our Lord Jesus Christ. Faithful is he that calleth you, who also will do it."

This is when **"One Heart"** was birthed, originally it was single-hearted. The revelation message found in the **"One Heart**

Series™" is a message from the heart of my Father(God) to me and to his children from afar and near to become ONE (united, whole, complete, entire, without fracture, or division). Moses led the children of Israel out of Egypt, but he could not take that out of them. Just as it was then, so it is today that it requires an individual relationship with the second Moses (Jesus). He has spoken to us and it has come to pass. Listen to the voice crying out loud "Receive Ye the Lord" and you shall have POWER to tread, walk, leap, break, command and deliver yourself! It is the focus of this series as we continue on to restore the lost and confused to the Shepherd! It has always been about 'A' Seed, 'One' Seed. He originally made us in HIS image, by the Godhead who were on one accord, therefore; no discord, separation, despair or competition was in the original Adam! They created us in their image, which is for us to walk in peace, wholeness, preservation, fullness and love! God has been crying out for the broekn-hearted to come home, and through my life He has chosen to speak to your heart! Come away with me on this journey to be with my Beloved and let us go into the Bride Grooms Chamber and the countryside where we can learn to skip, lead and dance!

CHAPTER 4

♥

CHRISTIAN, WHAT HINDERS YOU?

"The more afraid we are, the harder waiting becomes.
That is why waiting is such an unpopular attitude for many people."
Henri J.M. Nouwen

Christian, What Hinders You?

4- Christian, What Hinders You?

Removing a Primary Hindrance

ANGER: Word Study

Anger means affliction, grief, narrow, and to strangle. A strong feeling of displeasure and usually of antagonism, rage. (word study adapted from Zodhiates "The Complete Word Study Dictionary)

In Summary: Anger: means emotional excitement, (induced) by intense displeasure. Anger the most general term, names the reaction; but in itself conveys nothing about the intensity or the justification or manifestation of the emotional state of one who is angry.

Angere in (latin) = to strangle
Anchein in (Greek)= to strangle
Enge in (Old Eng.)= narrow
Angr in (Old Nor.)= grief

Anger   (Mid. Eng)= affliction

Synonym: according to Websters New Collegiate Dictionary means: one or more words or expressions of the same language that have the same or nearly the same meaning in some or all senses. Lets examine these synonyms of anger from Zodhiates; Complete Word Study Dictionary.

Ire

greater intensity with an evident display of feeling (color change).

Rage

loss of self-control from violence of emotion (screaming).

Fury

overmastering destructive rage merging on madness.

Indignation

stresses righteous anger at what one considers unfair, mean or shameful.

Wrath

imply either rage or indignation but is likely to suggest a desire or intent to revenge or punish.

Antonym as defined in Websters New Collegiate Dictionary is: a word of opposite meaning. (simple isn't it).

That is just how simple it is for us to walk opposite of the light, it is not the big sins that keep us from being blessed and entering into Heaven. It is the little, simple things that are chronic and repetitive in our lives that hinder us from running toward God. Instead we run away from him, thereby making us anathema (cursed and excommunicated) from HIS presence. We are either for and with him, or we are against and absent from him. If we are absent than we are anti-, and that means against; so if we are anti- against -- what? Christ.

No, no, no, she must have made a typographical error. Surely, she is not saying that if we are against and absent, we are Anti-Christ. Think again, it is true, earlier you read that Jesus thanked his Father, and commented that he had not lost any of his disciples, except the son of perdition. Perdition means, destruction, and utter destruction, and eternal damnation.

In the Book of Acts, Chapters 2 and 3; Peter clearly draws the line between those who are with and for God.

And the Bible, quotes Paul as having said that 'if they had been of us, then they would have remained!

Once we possess our souls and allow God to have the reins of our hearts which fuel anger, we can run the race that is set before us and run it with patience. Because as you begin the journey of salvation you will have many opportunities to be angry, but remember he desires for us to sin not!

Anger uncontrolled and lingered in opens the door for the adversary to bring about the works of the flesh. The strong man which was once bound, is given legal permission to become unfettered and bring in seven times more guests than what were there before. We must realize that there is a progression to ungodly anger that darkens the window of the soul! From anger, we enter into resentment, self-vendication, bitterness, grief, criticism, judgmentalism, envy and strife to name a few.

These reinforce anger like you would a dam with sandbags and allows it to rule in your heart. When anything besides the love and peace of God rules in your heart, you are on dangerous territory! He has made us free and we entangle ourselves again with the yoke of bondage. I have seen many disappointments and betrayals in my life, and have walked in anger and been made free, and walking free as he intended me to be. On this journey there will be opportunities to become distracted by rocks, pebbles, boulders, material possession, lifes issues and personal relationships. I use to argue with Paul about wishing that all men were single, so that their attention would be solely on God! Thought I could be every woman, have it all and still keep my attention on God, and prove allow Paul to have his opinion.

Only to discover that there was a definite truth to what he said! We can get distracted and in a brief moment lose valuable time on the clock if we stay too long at the fair!

What I mean is Satan will present you with what moves you and give you the opportunity to move! You can submit his present to God and resist it and he and it will have to be gone! But tarry there awhile and you will have sorrow! God has time, purpose and your season under control, but we must trust him, look at him as Jesus looked at him, with belief that he is well able to perform and watch over his word!

Many of us have boat loads of prophecies and words of knowledge that have been spoken to us on paper, cassette, video tape, and in our memory banks, and we are wondering when will it come to pass! Time and time goes by and we still hold on to what we have been told, rehearse, regurgitate it and share with anybody who will listen, and who hasn't heard it so many times that they lip sync the story while we are telling it to them. It is time for a change on every level of our lives and we must get off the throne of our lives and turn it over to the one who created us! Can the clay dictate to the potter, Jeremiah didn't think so, and we know it to be true ourselves. We are the workmanship of his hand!

You may be wondering what in the world this has to do

with being one-hearted. Well the Bible says if your eye be full of light, then your whole body is full of light. The kind of anger we examined most of us walk in and out of 100% of from time to time, and it is not of the light, but of the dark. So, if we are to be children of the light, we must walk in the light. And the light is Jesus Christ, who shines into our hearts through himself the word of God (His Father and those whom his Father has given him).

Jesus, told his Father, he had not lost one, except the son of perdition, whom his Father had given him. To walk in the Fruit of the Spirit, requires us to walk in newness of life and in his presence.

Testify! Holy Scriptures, maybe some of you have already gotten the revelation.

It is 'In His presence that there is fullness of joy, and treasures forever.' There is no darkness or deception in his presence.

Have you ever noticed the countenance change on an individual when they are angry, some get red, others get darker than their true color. (The gift of discernment will reveal things like this to you, so as to allow you to watch what you say and do, because the word of God in Proverbs; says that a soft answer turns away wrath, and that when you are in the company/way of a fool agree with them)

Know that we know that wrath is a degree of anger, we can walk circumspectly before God and man and not sin! When God gave me this revelation, he told me to imagine an oven with its' degree settings, the farther to the right on most ovens you go the cooler the temperature, and the farther to the left you go the hotter the temperature. Somebody, catch this revelation please !!! Even the worldly things mimic the things of God! Where is the hand of fellowship on God - It is on the right! And who is seated there, it is Jesus! And what is on his left hand - It is His Judgment! Are you ready to see what can happen when you allow Satan to turn the knob on your oven, away from the fellowship of the Father, Son and the Holy Spirit! Like kindling is fuel to a fire so this next one is to anger!

Impatience

Henri Nouwen, says that "A waiting person is a patient person. The word patience means the willingness to stay where we are and live the situation out to the full in the belief that something hidden there will manifest itself to us. Impatient people are always expecting the real thing to happen somewhere else and therefore want to go elsewhere. The moment is empty, but patient people dare to stay where they are. Patient living means to live actively in the present and wait there. Waiting, then, is not passive. It involves nurturing the moment, as a mother nurtures the child that is growing in her. Zechariah, Elizabeth, and Mary were very present to the moment. That is why they could hear the angel. They were alert, attentive to the voice that spoke to them and said, "Don't be afraid. Something is happening to you. Pay attention....Waiting is open-ended. Open-ended waiting is hard for us because we tend to wait for something very concrete, for something that we wish to have...But Zechariah, Elizabeth, and Mary were not filled with wishes. They were filled with hope...Hope is trusting that something will be fulfilled, but fulfilled according to the promises and not just according to our wishes...Mary was actually saying in the words, "I am the handmaid of the Lord...let what you have said be done to me" (Luke 1:38). She was saying, "I don't know what this all means, but I trust that good things will happen," She trusted so deeply that her waiting was open to all possibilities. And she did not want to control them. She believed that when she listened carefully, she could trust what was going to happen. To wait open-endedly is an enormously radical attitude toward life. So is to trust that something will happen to us that is far beyond our own imaginings. So, too is giving up control over our future and letting God define our life, trusting that God molds us according to God's love and not according to our fear...How do we wait?...Luke 1:39-56,...we wait together....something was happening to Elizabeth as well as to Mary...these two women...came together and enabled each other to wait...These two women created space for each other to wait. They affirmed for each other that something was happening that was worth waiting for....Prayer...is coming together around the promise...It is saying "thank you" for the seed that has been planted..."We are waiting for the Lord, who has already come."...Waiting in the knowledge that someone wants to address us. The question is, are we home? Are we at our address, ready to respond to the doorbell? We need to wait together, to keep each other at home spiritually, so that when the word comes it can become flesh in us." Like Paul and Silas waited together in prison, they were enabling each other, and where there are any two or three gathered together in my name, God says, he would be in their midst. There is no room for impatience on your journey. It will cause you not to be home, but down the street, and around the corner where you will miss your promise. Wait I say on the Lord and be of good courage, and again I say WAIT! While we are waiting on You Lord, let us address the static on the line in our hearts. A compass is only good when the conditions are right for it to determine directional center in my opinion.

Love and Hate

So too, if Love does not abound in our hearts, then hatred is creating havoc and causing us to be on shaky ground. Think about how much Jonah hated the ninevites, that he wanted to see them destroyed. He ran away from Gods' purpose only to find himself in chaos. Hatred is what the God of this world operates in, and when we are in hate we are on his domain! Satan was ascended on high and became lifted up in himself, and cast down (descended). Jesus came down from on high and descended into Satans' domain, and then ascended on High, so that we might ascend and be seated in heavenly places. We can not ascend when our hearts are full of dissension, discord and anarchy! Hatred among the brethren is a killer of enormous proportion. The love of God is to be shed abroad in our hearts, and we wait in earnest expectation! Breast to breast, cheek to cheek. Have we lost sight of the plan of God for the world, and brought the world into the sanctuary in our temples and forgot to not lift up our hands in wrath and doubting. Whose are we?

Hatred

There are opposing systems at work in the universe, and a few are righteousness and evil, and love and hate. In Volume I we scratched the surface of righteousness and evil. In this volume we will scratch the surface of love and hate.

In my research I stumbled onto works by Remy De Gourmont, and here is a quote I would like to share on the topic of "The Psychology of Hatred and Cruelty" he states "Poets and philosphers have written many books about love. It forms the nucleus of a religion that controls the universe. "If I speak with the tongues of men and of angels, but have not love, I am become sounding brass, or a clanging cymbal," writes the apostle to the Corinthians. One would believe that love constitutes the central force of existence, did not a deeper insight into life teach us that hate is the really great motive power of all that happens. There are special reasons why we confess our love and conceal the hatred...Close to God the Devil reigns. Near the heaven of love, the hell of hate. The Devil as the symbol of evil is also the symbol of hatred. He who hates professes himself the disciple of the Devil. Since every one strives for likeness to God and tends to develop beyond his actual ego to the ideal ego, he plays the part of a good man. The hatred is concealed; love is simulated if it is not present. As a result, we see a lying picture of the world, which exaggerates the significance of love and undervalues the importance of hate. We have taken a long time to grasp the law of bipolarity in its fundamental meaning: There is no love without hate! This principle is still easier to comprehend than its converse: There is no hatred without love. It is due to the possibility of reversing and displacing the affect that these two facts could remain so long unrecognized..."

But, we serve a God who will not let us be tempted above that which we can bear! Because He knows the way we take and the frame he has made for us to bear up. His yoke is easy and His burden is light! We have been deceived by Satan and taken on a false-burden onto our frame and a yoke of silver about our necks, that weigh us down and beset us. Let us lay aside every weight and sin that doth so easily beset us! Is hate hindering progression on your journey?

In the Encyclopedia of Human Emotions (Volume 1), the term Hate is defined as "referring to any intense dislike or hostility, whatever its object. Hate could be directed at a person, a group, an idea, some other abstraction, or an inanimate object." While Love in Volume 2, is defined as "a deep and tender feeling of affection for or attachment or devotion to a person or persons...a strong, usually passionate, affection of one person for another, bsed in part on sexual attraction...sexual passion....sexual intercourse....the contrasts between the tender and affectionate aspects of love on the one hand and the passionate and explosive aspects of love on the other."...

Colors of Love

Love can be characterized by six major styles: eros, ludus, storge, mania, agape and pragma.

1. Eros , characterized by physicality as well as a possible sense of the exotic, where the lover finds a beloved whose physical presentation of self embodies an image already held in the mind of the lover,
2. Ludus, referring to play-like or game-like love (based on the use of the term by Ovid),
3. Storge, characterized by slowly developing affection and companionship,
4. Mania, characterized by obsession, jealousy, and great emotional intensity,
5. Agape, a form of altruistic love found whne the lover views it as his or her duty to love without expectation or reciprocation, and
6. Pragma, a practical style of love involving conscious consideration of the demographic and other objective characteristics of the loved one."

Let's take a look at hate first:

Hatred of - Miso

Psalms 139: 21-22, which says: "Do I not hate them that hate you? I hate them with a perfect hatred." In the Greek: hate, hater, hatred; disgust for.

Hatred of knowledge - Misology

There are those who hate knowledge or learning and those who hate ideas. The latter being a misologist.

Hatred of Mankind - Misanthrope

A hatred or distrust of all people (mankind). A misanthrope is a man who always believes the worst of a person at first and never changes his mind. Hatred of, or aversion to, mankind. A profound morbid distrust of human beings individually and collectively. This includes ones mother, father or entire family.

Hatred of Men - Misandrist

One who hates men; especially, a woman and is consumed with a drive and belief that men are the source of all their troubles.

Hatred of Women - Misogyny

When there is a hatred of women present, more commonly there is found a correlation to events in childhood. Disdain for women is expressed similiarly by men and women and often can be seen in conflicts of homosexuality. When a homosexual male is passive he may hold sever disdain for women as a response to his own self-hatred of their gender.

Hatred of Children - Misopedia

Abhorring children, especially one's own, it may include the idea of incest with an unconscious viewing of the child as the consequence of incestuous relations.

Hatred of Marriage - Misogamy

Hating marriage or having an aversion to marriage.

In some psychiatric circles it is "often based on an unresolved Oedipus complex." It is likened to incest and misogamy is their defense against it.

In Summary of Hatred

To have any of the above-mentioned forms of hate in our hearts is a representative of Misotheist - God Hatred, becaust hate prevents the love of God from permeating your soul, spirit and body. It keeps up walls of separation within the heart of man that will not allow for unity of the faith and for love to flow from breat to breast. I speak of this first hand, because growing up in what I consider a religious home where there were demonstrations of things that were not always God inspired created a divided heart in my own life. Compartmentalized rooms, sealed doors and none with windows. In my spiritual eyes my heart was a land mine and a maze! The authority figures over me were untrustworthy, and unprotective of my wellfare. Growing up in this environment as a child creates suspicion, hypervigilance, distrust and aggressive or passive rebellion that carries down through adulthood if not addressed. Who doe can a child trust if not those who are in authority over them to care, nurture and protect them. Never mind who do you love and who will love you and who will be loyal and kind! What a world of disharmony and trauma this causes a child! It is the hope and assurance from above that we will call forth the anointing of the hammer and breaker anointing of God to demolish these walls erected in the silent cries of the wounded child within! Children from the past, present and future are being subjected to hideous acts of cruelty in some homes that are labeled as "Christian" - creating a feeling of hopelessness and despair. Without hope children are underdeveloped emotionally and intellectually. As they go through puberty onto adolescence feeling defenseless, not knowing that God has a bounty attached to the wickedness done to them and anyone who dares to offend them will be repaid by God! This is a subject that is near and dear to my heart, and sends a cry out into my spirit to children, and to to the adult who still has a wounded child inside of them that God is ABLE!!!!! Oh yes, He is, able to deliver, save and set free from the hatred, bitterness, grief, pain, neglect, abuse and trauma of your childhood! Abuse comes in many forms, some of which we will scratch the surface during this discourse.

In Summary of Love

Perfect Love Cast Out All Fear. God Is Love. What man says that he loves God and hates his brother. The Love of God is shed abroad from breast to breast and cheek to cheek. How then shall men know that ye are my disciples, if ye have love one for another. Love does not seek its own, is not puffed up, vaunteth not itself.....

When we are not walking in love towards ourselves and others we are walking in the realm and pathway of abuse!

Abuse - Abnormal Use

How is abuse inflicted upon ourselves, by ourselves and by others and what we do in response to having been abused?

Self-Love - Narcissism

An exceptional interest in and admiration for yourself. Narcissism is the pattern of characteristics and behaviors which involve infatuation and obsession with one's self to the exclusion of others and the egotistic and ruthless pursuit of one's gratification, dominance and ambition. In everyday use outside the field of psychology, the word generally refers to people who just are inordinately fond of themselves, without the pathological connotations. A compulsion and stimulation with one's own body, to the point of making a person incapable and/or limited in their ability to experience fulfilling sexual and social relationships. There are said to be plus or minus 1% of the population who exhibit these tendencies and 75% of that are men.)

In scholarly circles it is believed that the onset of narcissism is in infancy, childhood and early adolescence; abuse and trauma suffered at the hands of parents or those in authority, including those of their own age. There are two types or categories; Cerebral and Somatic. The cerebral narcissist is intelligent and derives fulfillment from their achievements, while the somatic narcissist fulfillment comes from physical appearance and success. My purpose in mentioning narcissism is to build a framework for understanding the psychological damage most of the people in the world have suffered, and how these damages affect them in their vertical relationship with God and their horizontal relationships with mankind. Feelings of self-importance, exaggerated successes, embellishment, and fantasies of god-likeness to their physical appearance.

We will need to understand this one thing that there is a conflict that exist in the world/universe. The conflict of righteousness and unrighteousness, love and hatred, self and God. It is the conflict of self that is the central theme I want to draw you into. If we are not pleasing to God in our ways, then we must be pleasing to someone or ourselves. It is the love of self that keeps us from growing up into the unity of the faith. As mature believers we are easily entreated or should be, as sinners in need of salvation we were not and are not so easily entreated. The core of what drives us are the five senses. We use these to bring about self-gratification in whatever form we care to experience, lawlessly or lasciviously.

In Christ we seek to bring self under subjection to Gods' authority, and self does not always go along quietly with the plan of transformation. Let's approach this part of our journey examining the cycle of abuse.

Emotional

It involves two categories of people: The abuser and the abused. It is the use of verbal or nonverbal acts that hurt or threaten physical or psychological harm. Verbal acts such as criticizing, belittling remarks, screaming, scolding, ignoring and tearing down and badgering. Nonverbal acts include destroying personal belongings, hurting family, friends, pets or limiting access to resources such as money, and isolation and usually occurs in private. Wounded children grow up and become wounded adults.

As a child I was abused emotionally, physically, sexually, mentally and spiritually even up to a portion of my adult life. It is the emotional abuse that cut to the center of my being and did the most damage in my life. My approach is fom the view point of a child.

Let's read Psalms 39, "I said, "I will guard my ways That I may not sin with my tongue; I will guard my mouth as with a muzzle While the wicked are in my presence." I was mute and silent, I refrained {even} from good, And my sorrow grew worse. My heart was hot within me, While I was musing the fire burned; {Then} I spoke with my tongue: "LORD, make me to know my end And what is the extent of my days; Let me know how transient I am. "Behold, You have made my days {as} handbreadths, And my lifetime as nothing in Your sight; Surely every man at his best is a mere breath. Selah. "Surely every man walks about as a phantom; Surely they make an uproar for nothing; He amasses {riches} and does not know who will gather them. "And now, Lord, for what do I wait? My hope is in You. Deliver me from all my transgressions; Make me not the reproach of the foolish. "I have become mute, I do not open my mouth, Because it is You who have done {it.} Remove your plague from me, Because of the opposition of Your hand I am perishing. With reproofs You chasten a man for iniquity; You consume as a moth what is precious to him; Surely every man is a mere breath. Selah. "Hear my prayer, O LORD, and give ear to my cry; Do not be silent at my tears; For I am a stranger with You, A sojourner like all my fathers. Turn Your gaze away from me, tht I may smile {again} Before I depart and am no more."

David expresses the nothingness of his self and declares that he is in need of Gods' guidance out of all his transgressions. The law was made for the transgressor, and David was notorious for breaking the law and notorious for repenting and crying out to God. There is a Second David who has come and walked uprightly before his father and subdued self unto death. This is what must be done with us, we are not asked to die physically as Christ died, but to die spiritually to the deeds and desires of the flesh of self! Deliverance is nigh you even in your mouth! Simply speak the word and deliverance comes in! Nothing in heaven moves except in response to the Word of God and prayer! The

Angels of Heaven watch over tha word to perform it! You speak the Word, as Cornelius told Jesus that if he would speak the word only he knew that it would be done! That is deliverance that is available to you right now. It is not about a feeling, but knowing in whom you believe and what you believe. Are you ready to go further down the road road called "oneness"? I want to interject this sampling on Post-Traumatic Stress - not as a medical diagnosis, but as a point of discussion, because many of us have never gone away to war, but have waged war on home territory. Selah - Pause and Think About It.

Post Traumatic Stress

"Source: PTSD As Contained In The 4th Edition, Text Revision (DSM-IV-TR) 7 And Focuses On Diagnosis And Management, Including The Detection And Treatment Of Comorbidities.

PTSD aka Da Costa syndrome ("soldier's heart"), the psychological effects of trauma have been described throughout military history. **Soldiers heart** is characterized by cardiac symptoms associated with irritability and increased arousal, in veterans of the American Civil War...it was hypothesized that "shell shock" resulted from brain trauma caused by exploding shells...terms such as "combat neurosis" and "operational fatigue" were used to describe combat-related symptoms.

PTSD may be caused by exposure to a severe traumatic stress that threatens death or serious injury or threat to personal integrity, as follows:

Rape

Sexual and physical abuse

Car accidents

Fires and being in a war zone

Receiving a serious medical diagnosis

Being subjected to invasive painful treatment of medical problems

A number of factors increase the likelihood that a child will develop PTSD in response to a given stress, including the following.

Lack of social and parental support

Prior exposure to traumatic incidents

A preexisting psychiatric disorder

Repeated trauma

Trauma caused by a person (especially if by a trusted caregiver) rather than resulting from an accident

Parental reaction is a critical factor affecting the child's reaction. Parents' anxiety and difficulty coping with life as the result of the trauma may overwhelm a child, while parental ability to cope and provide a safe haven for a child may markedly affect the child's ability to deal with the stressor or the propensity to develop protracted PTSD."

The war torn ravages of your soul, your mind, will and emotions react the same as if you had fought in one of the military wars. Because we are in a war, and we wrestle not against flesh and blood, but against principalities, powers, rulers of darkness and spiritual wickendness in high places. The only wise God our savior has made a way of escape for us from the war trauma of the soul realm into the marvelous light of the Holy Spirit. You have felt untied, disconnected and dysfunctional long enough. Let's confront the aftermath of sin and its penalty with the Word, the Blood, and the Spirit! We must now go before his throne and receive symphony! Rest!

Symphony "Sumphonos"

We must become united, "echad" with God to go further. Lets' stop and examine another word "Sumphonos" looks familiar doesn't it. This is the birth of "Symphony" - to be like minded, agreeing and on one accord. Can you imagine a self-serving symphony? They would not last very long, clearly the Bible says that a house divided against itself can not stand! A symphony orchestra divided can not perform or make a symphonic sound!

To be "asumphonos" is to disagree. Again, we see in the book of Amos, that it states, how can two walk together except they agree! Agreement is needed for togetherness, and a symphonic walk! We are sojourners in a land that is not ours as believers.

Journey

Means to go away from ones own country, people, and/or travel abroad. (Matthew 21:33) Travel from the old to the new "poreuomai" - meaning to transport onesel from one place to another. To "sunodeuo" - to be on the way with someone, to travel or journey with.

On this journey towards oneness we are transporting ourselves from one place to another; from the old to the new. The old involves the part of your life from conception to conversion.

The new encompasses the conversion experience through the transformation process. I say conversion is an experience because it only requires a willingness to accept what is being presented to you as a part of your world. Transformation requires effort beyond experience, that will not always be in agreement with what you believe or feel like doing, but if you are to remain in agreement and walk together with God, you will have to subject yourself to his authority as David did in Psalms 39. Flesh does not want to die, but to be successful on your journey you must walk like God says we must walk in his Word!

Trans -

Means to bridge. The Word of God, Jesus and the Holy Spirit are your bridge from the old to the new way of life! This volume approaches the baggage of conception and the environment of the womb that have been wrapped in flesh in the person of you. It is who you are today, as you read this book. That moment of time and the experiences of life have made you who you are and that person needs transformation. We have moved past the point of conversion and are ready to work out our soul salvation in fear and trembling. Transformation takes work! We are transformed by the renewing of our minds. Bridged across by faith, looking unto Jesus the author and finisher of our faith as in Hebrews 12:2.

The Bible says that we are shapen in iniquity (Psalms 51). Shapen in lawlessness that would place us in broken fellowship with man and God immediately upon entry int the world at birth.

We look at ultrasounds and sonograms and see pictures of the outer man that is being shapen in the womb, but we can not see the inner man and its desperately wicked heart! How angelic that baby looks inside of the mothers womb. Within the heart of that angelic looking being is the sin nature of the fallen Adam. I do still believe that a baby can be born into this world indwelled by the Holy Spirt as John the Baptist was. I did not have this revelation when I was carrying my child, because I would have pursued this with all that was within me. God is the same yesterday, today and forever more.

Surely it would require a life of oneness on the mothers' part to create the environment that would allow the Holy Spirit total access to her whole soul, mind and body to press into the place of divine infiltration.

Praise God who is able to do exceedingly and abundantly above all that we may ask or think. Come away with me into the mountains and into the bedchamber of the bridegroom and let us be as one!

In Volume I we broke the fallow ground as you would before you prepare to plant a garden. In Volume II we will shovel, pick axe, stump pull, rock extract and cultivate the soil of your heart to go deeper so that you may go higher. I witnessed two oak trees growing in the same neighborhood. One has a wide trunk and small acorns, with a root system on top of the ground growing in a wide space. And then another growing in a restricted place, with no roots above ground and acorns the size of small eggs. God spoke to my heart and said that the latter grew acorn like eggs, because its root system was deeper and the limbs could bear the weight of the heavier fruit. Also, that its deep roots came about as a result of it being in a restricted triangular space. This is the new day of runners on this journey. God is about to shift, if not already shifted by the time you read this book, his focus to his sons and daughters who have had to come up in restricted places. Never enough to do what was in your heart, but you did all you could do with what you had in your hands. You took a little and made it multiply, you served in confined places with gladness and obedience! Child of God, you have not been forgotten. Look as far as your eyes can see, and then look through the eyes of God and possess the land! Your season, your day, your hour, your moment , your turn has risen upon you like the Holy Spirit rose and hovered over Mary and impregrnated her! Now the Holy Spirit is brooding over you and about to bring forth, water in a dry place, fruit in a barren place, oil in a crushing place, and corn in an empty place. Feel it, taste it, smell it in the atmosphere! You are so close that you can sense it coming up behind you, you want to look back and around you because it feels as if something or someone is walking up on you. Yes! YES! And YES! If I could type in tongues, I would tell you what my spirit is saying right now! I can hardly type for the unction and utterance that is ruminating inside of my spirit! Crying out prepare ye the way of the Lord! He is high and lifted up and his train has filled the temple! God breaking out on the North, South, East and West - breaking us out of lack, out of obscurity and placing you on a journey that you have waited on in expectancy all of your born again life! Whew! Halleluia!

Praise Him, because he is able to do exceedingly and abundantly above all that we may ask or think!

CHAPTER 5
♥
Y-INTERSECTION

Y-Intersection

5- Y-Intersection

The "Y" formation in a highway is created at the top of the leg of the "Y". We often see this type of intersection where a chasm exist between the left and the right side of the intersection. The amusing thing is that sometimes no matter which leg you take you end up at the same destination or geographic area, but on opposing sides of the highway. The choice we make to serve God or Satan is what I want us to reflect on as a divided heart. Just as a neighbor can live across the street in the same community and have two different zip codes. This is how we often find ourselves traveling on the road of Christianity! We get in the general vicinity of righteousness, but divided by issues of the heart.

How does this get accomplished in the spirit realm? Much the same way as it does on the highway. You make the choice to take the left or the right side of the intersection at the bottom of the "Y". Let's call that the place of decision or commitment! Will you commit to follow God or Satan, today?

Remember, Solomon says in Ecclesiates "A wise man's heart is at his right hand; but a fool's heart at his left." Let's apply this spiritual law to ourselves as we continue our journey. In Volume 1 of this Series, we looked at the fall of man, the condition, the restoration of mans' relationship with God to, himself and others. In Volume 2, we are going to examine ourselves and the light of Gods Word closer to see what has kept us from walking "With Oneness of Heart" before God and man!

We must look to ourselves as the culprit of why we have not seen the success God has ordained for us in our lives. What are we doing in our Physical, Spiritual, Emotional and Social lives that hinder us from walking in the victory he desires for us to walk in. Let me say that the success I am speaking of is not about things and stuff! It is the success of walking worthy of your calling as God has asked us to.

Maybe success for one is not a fit all for everyone. The success we want to focus on is what was found in 3 John. Being in balance in every area that he has called us to. In Galatians 5:1 we are commanded to "STAND FAST therefore in the liberty wherewith Christ hath made us free, and be not entangled again with the yoke of bondage." In Philippians 1:6, "Being confident of this very thing, that he which hath begun a good work in you will perform it until the day of Jesus Christ:." Because we are doing this, "...take no thought, saying, What shall we eat? Or, What shall we drink? Or, Wherewithal shall we be clothed? (For after these things do the Gentiles seek) for your heavenly Father knoweth that ye shall have need of all these things. But seek ye first the kingdom of God, and his righteousness; and all these things shall be added unto you."

For Length of Days

Because David has instructed us in Psalms 39:4, "Lord, make me to know mine end, and the measure of my days, what it is; that I may know how frail I am." And in I Thessalonians 5:8-10,23-24 "But let us, who are of the day, be sober, putting on the breastplate of faith and love; and for an helmet, the hope of salvation. For God hath not appointed us to wrath, but to obtain salvation by our Lord Jesus Christ. Who died for us, that, whether we wake or sleep, we should live together with him." In v 23-24, "And the very God of peace sanctify you wholly; and I pray God your whole spirit and soul and body be preserved blameless unto the coming of our Lord Jesus Christ. Faithful is he that calleth you, who also will do it."

Measured

Now the success that we will seek after is to do as he has commanded us in the time God has measured out for us in the earth, and as we follow in this path all the other things will be added unto us! Never say that God is a liar or unfaithful, because it is not so! He is not capable of being unfaithful or a liar. As a songwriter penned the words of Pontius Pilate "I Find no Fault in Him." Neither do I! What has transpired or not manifested in my life is of my own doing, and the blame is in wandering aimlessly without a head in the state of "Ichabod". Having myself as my ruler and not the one who created me before the foundation of the world. I intend to share with you the areas that we find ourselves in at the bottom of the "Y-intersection" unable to decide which way to take. Not to be redundant, but let's for the sake of the scriptures let us use Ecclesiates, as our compass.

CHAPTER 6

♥

OUR COMPASS

"Love Suffers Long And Is Kind?Is Not Provoked? Endures All Things." I Corinthians 13:4-7 Nkjv

President William McKinley had been pressed upon and attacked by a poor young reporter on numerous occasions. This reporter did not have a winter coat, and he observed him shivering one night outside of his coach. Mr. McKinley stopped and put his overcoat on him and invited him to ride inside of his coach. The reporter replied to his kindness, that he (Mr. McKinley) did not know who he was, I am the one who has been attacking you. Mr. McKinley responded telling the young reporter that he knew who he was, and still proceeded to invite him into the coach and give him his coat. This is a demonstration of blessing those who persecute you at its' finest. How many of us will respond when in a similar situation. Father; help us to be more like you and less like ourselves! Love is Our Compass! God is Love!

Our Compass

6 – Our Compass (God's Hands)

The passage as our directional pointer on this journey is; **"A wise man's heart is at his right hand**; but a fool's heart at his left." The right hand of God is used as the hand of His **power,** our **pleasures,** to **hold us** up, to **embrace us,** the **sheep are on the right** (goats on the left), he **exalts (promotion)** with it and **Jesus stands and sits** there! And **wisdom holds the length of our days** in her right hand! Above all **righteousness is in his right** hand! Here are the scriptures that bare this out:

Power

St Mark 14:62 "And Jesus said, **I am:** and ye shall see the Son of man sitting on the right hand of **power**, and coming in the clouds of heaven."

Pleasure

Psalms 16:11 "Thou wilt show me the path of life: in thy presence is fulness of joy; at thy right hand there are **pleasures** for evermore."

Hold Us

Psalms 18:35 "Thou hast also given me the shield of thy salvation: and thy right hand hath **holden me up**, and thy gentleness hath made me great."

Embrace Us

Solomon 2:6 "His left hand is under my head, and his right hand doth **embrace me**."

Sheep or Goat

Matthew 25:32-33 "And before him shall be gathered all nations: and he shall separate them one from another, as a shepherd divideth his sheep from his goats: And he shall **set the sheep on the right hand**, but the **goats on the left**."

Seated

St. Mark 16:19 "So then after the Lord had spoken unto them, he was received up into heaven, and **sat on the right hand of God**."

Standing Up

At the stoning of Stephen in Acts 7:54-55 "When they heard these things, they were cut to the heart, and they gnashed on him with their teeth." But he, (Stephen) **being full** of the Holy Ghost, looked up steadfastly into heaven, and saw the glory of God, and Jesus **standing on the right hand of God**, And said, Behold, I see the heavens opened, and **the Son of man standing, (and not seated) on the right hand of God**." It is something when the son of God stands up for you!

Exalted/Promotion

Acts 2:32-35 "This Jesus hath God raised up, whereof we all are witnesses. Therefore **being by the right hand of God exalted**, and having received of the Father the promise of the Holy Ghost, he hath shed forth this, which ye now see and hear.

For David is not ascended into the heavens: but he saith himself, the Lord said unto my Lord, **Sit thou at my right hand**, Until I make thy foes they footstool."

Length of Life

Proverbs 3:16 speaks not of God, but of what Wisdom holds in her right hand, "**Length of days** is in her right hand: and in her left hand riches and honour." But in reference **to God the left hand** speaks of judgment. Scripture records in Proverbs that Wisdom is the principle thing! Psalms 48:10 "According to thy name, O God, so is thy praise unto the ends of the earth: thy **right hand is full of righteousness**."

Which hand should we choose! We choose the face of God to follow after on our journey to oneness. You decide?

Which Hand Do We Choose?

Now are we ready to use Ecclesiates, as our compass and this passage from there as our directional pointer on this journey; **"A wise man's heart is at his right hand**; but a fool's heart at his left."

Since we are Spirit beings living in a natural body, let's begin with the condition of our Spirits as the culprit our success or failure. In summary the word "Let" is to give permission or opportunity. The condition of our spirit will either let us advance or keep us back or destroy our success! Let also means to permit or enter, proceed or depart, to release from or as if from confinement, something that hinders; an obstacle, a retarding; hindrance; impediment; delay. "Consider whether your doings be to the let of your salvation or not." (Latimer quoted in Webster's Revised Unabridged Dictionary, 1996)

CHAPTER 7

♥

LET: WORD STUDY

Let: Word Study

7 – Let: Word Study

I have found during this journey that this small 3 letter word packs a punch in the way we have been dealt with and how we deal with others.

For this reason, I want to spend some time on this word's synonyms and antonyms.

Here are a few of the synonyms from Roget's New Millennium Thesaurus, First Edition, 2004.

Adopt	Keep	Stick with
Cherish	Maintain	Support
Claim	Possess	Take up
Continue	Pursue	
Defend	Retain	

When looking at the synonyms I think of the power of Gods Word in the scriptures where a picture is painted of us as we receive the Spirit of Adoption whereby we cry ABBA DADDY! We are cherished by God as the Apple of his eye! We have been claimed as children of God. We continue from faith to faith and from glory to glory! God is our rock and defense! He who keeps us neither slumbers nor sleeps! We are maintained by the banner that flies over us as proof of his love for us and our victory! We possess the gift of God which is Salvation and a promise of a heavenly home.

God pursues us with his eyes looking to and fro in the earth looking to show himself strong on our behalf! He retains the power over death, hell and the grave! He is a friend that sticks closer than a brother! He upholds us with his right hand! When our mother and our father forsakes us he takes up our cause! All of this in the little word "Let"!

For this purpose I chose to take one of the antonyms of let, "abandon" and examine its' synonyms. When I did this they painted a picture of the heartbreak many of us have endured in our lives!

Listed are 46 synonyms that I selected from the word **abandon**, which is an antonym of "Let" taken from the same source above. Those that stick out profoundly reflect how many people feel when they have been abandoned:

Abdicate	Deep Six	Drop
Back Out	Desert	Drop Out
Bail Out	Discard	Duck
Bow Out	Discontinue	Dump
Cast Off	Disown	Dust
Chicken Out	Ditch	Forsake
Cop Out	Drift Away	Give Up
Cut Loose		Kiss Goodbye

Lay Aside	Relinquish	Throw Over
Leave	Renounce	Overboard
Leave Behind	Ship Out	Toss Over
Let Go	Slide	Vacate
Pull Out	Stop	Walk
Quit	Storm Out	Withdraw
Reject	Strand	Yield
	Surrender	

These words are full of **negativity** and are reminders of things that have happened in the lives of those God redeemed to send to those who are bound!

Many of us have all known someone or been that person who has been the receiver or giver of the actions behind these words. And God has such a desire to have us apply the balm of gilead to these areas, and know that healing is already ours. We simply must walk out of infirmity and into healing as we meditate on the scriptures that apply to healing and believe that we receive it in our hearts without wavering or doubting. We will be confronted with pangs, pains, symptoms and manifestions of those diseases as we step out on faith like never before, but as our faith rises to the level of the word we have ignition and miracles happen. Like going to the fair and striking the mallet on the lever at the bottom of the tall gauge releases enough force to reach the bell at the top and ring it. So it is with the word of God, hit it with enough force (meditation and fasting) and it will rise to the level of expectancy we have in Gods' willingness to see us as healed! When your faith matches the level of the Word of God, a flame ignites and the power of God to perform a thing is accomplished in us. In Jeremiah 1:12, God says that he will hasten at his word to perform it. His word does not return unto him void. It is like a match head being struck on the side of a matchbox, and the sound of ignition is heard before the flame appears. The sound of healing is like that to me, we hear it before we see it manifest. Faith comes by hearing and hearing by the word of God! Healing is after all the childrens' bread! We are are one strike away from the greatest outpouring the 21st century church has ever seen! Can't you hear the sound of an abundance of rain?

CHAPTER 8

♥

OVERCOMERS
To The RIGHT

"May the shadow of the wings of the Most High be for ever the dwelling-place' of you all, who with oneness of heart occupy one home? father and mother, bound in the same brotherhood with your sons, being all the children of the one Father. Remember us. " Excerpt from Letter 101 (A.D. 409) From Augustine to Memor

Overcomers to the Right

8 – Overcomers to the Right

But LOOK AT WHAT GOD HAS DONE FOR US!

He has broken the power of death, hell and the grave off of our lives through the gift of his Son for us! He has descended and then ascended, so that we could be seated in heavenly places! It is the aim of this Volume is to take the redemptive, empowering and word of God amd apply it to the residue that has been left behind in our gardens under the soles of our feet! Let us place this residue under the soles of our feet for good! I am reminded of the anger, bitterness, grief and rebellion that I have embraced and experienced in my heart and life! What must we do to walk in the liberty that is ours? We must face the issues and the matters of our hearts and the evil feelings they stir up inside of us!

We are required to walk and not be weary, run and not faint because it is writtten that "WHEREFORE SEEING we also are compassed about with so great a cloud of witnesses, let us lay aside every weight, and the sin which doth so easily beset us, and let us run with patience the race that is set before us,

Looking unto Jesus the author and finisher of our faith; who for the joy that was set before him endured the cross, despising the shame, and is set down at the right hand of the throne of God." (Hebrews 12:1-2) The journey has began, and it is not how you begin that matters but how you finish!

He Chose Us Over Joy

The scripture records that Jesus "…who for the joy that was set before him endured the cross, despising the shame…" He was given a choice to call legions of angels to his assistance or complete the race that was set before him, and he did it with joy in the face of the joy of heaven that was his even if he had chosen not to finish the race God would have allowed him to quit!

Jesus already had everything under heaven and in heaven, he did not lay down his life for himself and his reward, but for ours! So that he would author and finish our faith. He is the beginning of our faith and the end of our faith during the race of our length of days! He is the center of our faith also, because he became our advocate and high priest ever making intercession for us as he is seated on the right hand of God! How do we remain seated with him as a joint heir with Christ Jesus! To sit down is to enter into the rest of God! We will deal with this later in the series! Meanwhile, let us deal with what is before us. We have to make a choice to live committed to God for the length of days in righteousness!

We are more than conquerors, we are OVERCOMERS, because our robe has been washed in the blood of the lamb.

The blood of the lamb was shed, and sprinkled on the mercy seat of heaven for the remissions of sin and ransom of man!

Have a Seat Over All Things

We remain seated by moving past the death, burial and resurrection of Jesus Christ! He has done so much more than that for us! We deny the power of what he has done when we fail to apply the Ascencion of his work!

Ephesians 4:7-16:

"But unto every one of us is given grace according to the measure of the gift of Christ. Wherefore he saith, When he ascended up on high, he led captivity captive, and gave gifts unto men.

(Now that he ascended, what is it but that he also descended first into the lower parts of the earth?

He that descended is the same also that ascended up far above all heavens, that he might **fill all things**.)

And he gave some, apostles; and some, prophets; and some, evangelists: and some, pastors and teachers;

For the perfecting of the saints, for the work of he ministry, for the edifying of the body of Christ:

Till we all come in the unity of the faith, and of the knowledge of the Son of God, unto a perfect man, unto the measure of the stature of the fulness of Christ:

That we henceforth be **no more** children, <u>tossed</u> to and fro, and <u>carried</u> about with every wind of doctrine, **by the sleight of men,** and **cunning craftiness**, whereby <u>they lie in wait</u> **to decieve**;

But speaking the truth in love, may **grow up** <u>into him</u> **all** things, which is the head, even Christ:

From whom the whole <u>body</u> fitly joined <u>together</u> and <u>compacted</u> by that which **every joint supplieth, according** to the <u>effectual working</u> in the <u>measure of every part</u>, **maketh increase** of the body unto the **edifiying of itself in love.**"

He Went Down To Get Us and Up to Seat Us

If he had not ascended into heaven we would still be lost! He ascended to sprinkle the blood on the mercy seat restoring unity in heaven by restoring the water of life and the tree of life that had been defiled in the Garden of Eden! He took what had been holding us captive, and took it captive and restored us to our proper place. Thus restoring balance in the earth and for all of those who are whosoever wills, even let them come!

While John was on the Isle of Patmos it is recorded that "AND HE showed me, a pure river of water of life, clear as crystal, proceeding out of the throne of God and of the Lamb. In the midst of the street of it, and on either side of the river, was there the tree of life, which bare twelve manner of fruits, and yielded her fruit every month: and the leaves of the tree were for the healing of the nations." (Revelations 22:1-2) Could this have been a fig tree?

Since he has reconciled the record books of heaven; what shall we say? Are more than conquerors through Christ Jesus! Shall we pursue and take back what the Devil has stolen from our generations past and present, and what he seeks to steal in the future!

CHAPTER 9

♥

WHEN HE SAID PURSUE; DID WE PURSUE?

When He Said Pursue, Did We...

9 – When He Said Pursue, Did We Pursue?

What shall we pursue? Our pursuit is for Gods' face and not his hand! If we do this all things will be added unto us, we are not to worship at the hand of God but the Face of God! He wants us to have things, but not for them to have us! Revelations 21:2-8 tells us of the divine success we are to pursue!

And I John saw the holy city, new Jerusalem, coming down from God out of heaven, prepared as a bride adorned for her husband, And I heard a great voice out of heaven saying, Behold, the tabernacle of God is with men, and he will dwell with them, and they shall be his people, and God himself shall be with them, and be their God. And God shall wipe away all tears from their eyes; and there shall be no more death, neither sorrow,

nor crying, neither shall there by any more pain:

for the former things are passed away.

And he that sat upon the throne said, Behold, I make all

things new. And he said unto me, Write: for these words are true and faithful.

And he said unto me, It is done. I am Alpha and Omega,

the beginning and the end. I will give unto him that is athirst of the fountain of the water of life freely. We are the sheep of his pasture and we have a shepherd that will not make us carry the weight of the sin of the first Adam any longer!

Sheep or Goat

God says that to He that overcometh shall inherit all things; and I will be his God and he shall be my son.

But the fearful, and unbelieving, and the abominable, and murderers, and whoremongers, and sorcerers, and idolaters, and all liars, shall have their part in the lake which burneth with fire and brimstone: which is the second death." From Verse 2-7 we find those who will be on the right hand of God the (sheep) those who have succeeded the righteous way.

Here we are again at the "Y-intersection" waiting to make a commitment to take the path that leads us away from Verse 8.

Because Verse 8 on the left hand of God are the (goats) who have succeeded in the unrighteous way: This is nothing to be envious or jealous of! They are the fearful, unbelieving, abominable, murderers, whoremongers, sorecers, idolaters, and all liars. These shall have their part in the lake which burneth with fire and brimstone: which is the second death.

Let us put away childishness and let us run this race with patience and endurance.

CHAPTER 10
OH GROW UP!

Oh Grow Up!

10 – Oh, Grow Up!

What is even more eye opening is the fact that many of us who say we believe find ourselves in the position of the goats far too frequently. We move in and out of the left and right side of the throne when we are tossed to and fro like children!

He has asked us this -- that we henceforth be: **no more children,** <u>tossed</u> **to and fro,** <u>carried</u> **about with every wind of doctrine,** by the sleight of men, *

and cunning craftiness, whereby <u>they lie in wait</u> **to decieve**; But speaking the truth in love, may grow up <u>into him</u> **all** things, which is the head, even Christ: We are affected in our inner man when we are lingering in childhood! To affect is to strive after or influence, produce a change in, to move to stir the emotions. The synonym implies the producing of an affect strong enough to evoke a reaction in thought, nature or behavior!

*The Sleight of Men:

When we are sleighted, this deals with the mistreatments, isolation and ostracizing by others that have caused us to become wounded. I find this amazing. These were things that were done to us, many of the things were beyond our control happening to us as children. God is saying to us that he knows what we/you have been through, and who did things to wound us, BUT don't let or allow those things to place you as a goat at Gods' left hand of judgement! He has made a way of escape for us to move past those hurtful words and actions when he led captivity captive!

Eviction Time

The words of sleight have turned into actions that we repeat in our daily lives! It has been long enough that words of negativity have been stalking, tormenting, and occupying our brain cells like phantoms, vagrants and trespassers!

Assignment

Take the time out to look up each one of these words and make a set of Flash Cards with a brief definition on the card and keep them before you to remind yourself that this is how we tend to behave when we allow the sleight of men to wound us and take up space in our behaviour towards ourselves, our loved ones and our destiny! It is time to EVICT! Lets classify these words and see how they play roles in our everyday reactions.

React

Number 1 through 12 is what we have now made our reactional behavior when we feel abandoned or rejected. We concede defeat as the only way out or we sabotage those who have hurt us as an act of revenge. Use Luke 1:68-79 to shed light further on our reactions to having experienced these actions:

Abdicate	Cast Off	Deep Six
Back Out	Chicken Out	Desert
Bail Out	Cop Out	Discard
Bow Out	Cut Loose	Discontinue

Relate

The next eleven reflect our relational behavior when we feel abandoned or rejected. These are what we act out when we have been abandoned or rejected. Create flash cards for these and use II Corinthians 3:2-3 as the light of the Word for counteracting these words.

Disown	Drop Out	Forsake
Ditch	Duck	Give Up
Drift Away	Dump	Kiss Goodbye
Drop	Dust	

Respond

And the final set of 22 words is what we have now made a part of how our dream and goal responsive behavior when we feel abandoned or rejected. We will repeatedly do these things to our dreams, goals and relationships. Use Psalms 51 as the light of the Word for counteracting these words:

Lay Aside	Quit	Renounce	Strand
Leave	Reject	Ship Out	Surrender
Leave Behind	Walk	Slide	Throw Over
Let Go	Withdraw	Stop	Throw Overboard
Pull Out	Yield	Storm Out	Toss Over
Vacate	Relinquish		

Now it is time to identify and address each one that you recognize in your life and counter attack them with the word of God! He that overcometh shall inherit all things; and I will be his God and he shall be my son. **All** of the <u>words </u>we just looked up for "Let & Abandon" are rooted in being fearful, unbelieving, abominable, murderers, whoremongers, sorcerers, idolaters, and liars. **All** of <u>these</u> shall have their part in the lake which burneth with fire and brimstone: which is the second death." From Verse 2-7 are those who will be on the right hand of God the (sheep) those who have succeeded the righteous way. As an act of practicing the presence of God use the flash cards as a point of contact to keep before your face, and as behavior that Gods' face smiles on. Additionally, add on a flash card this scripture - Romans 8:35,and let's begin tossing out the old mans nature and the former things by replacing them with the word of God and the things that are of good report!

CHAPTER 11

♥

HOW To MAKE ROOM FOR ONE MORE

"May the shadow of the wings of the Most High be for ever the dwelling-place' of you all, who with oneness of heart occupy one home? Father and mother, bound in the same brotherhood with your sons, being all the children of the one Father. Remember us."
Excerpt from Letter 101 (A.D. 409)
From Augustine to Memor

How to Make Room for One More

11- How to Make Room for One More

As with any birth, an environment must be created that will support, nurture and cultivate a new life. Refer back to Chapters II & III of Volume I, the roles and relationships of the man and woman. A man can not make room for a "Woman of God" if he is dangling between what his identity is as a man. Likewise a woman can not make room for a "Man of God" if she is dangling between identities.

At this point we are going to do a brief word study of this title. The word MAKE means to seem to begin, to cause to happen, or to be experienced or appear to favor the growth or occurrence of, to fit, intend or destine by or as if by creating, to lay out, construct, to frame or formulate in the mind, to set in order.

The word ROOM means in its Latin origin -- open land rendered in English as an extent of space occupied by or sufficient or available for something.

The word **FOR** is used to indicate a purpose or goal, used as a function word to indicate duration of time or extent of space.

A Great Little Fixer Upper

FOR SALE BY OWNER
Terms of Contract
Opt. A) As is 100k
Opt. B) As is 100k,
    You finance
Opt. C) Move-in 95k,
    Owner to repair

What do you notice about the condition of this house?
Broken windows, torn drapes, hole in roof, cracked walls, sidewalk and foundation.

(c) Patricia E. Adams

Now we must lay aside every weight, Hebrews 12:1, so that we can enlarge our space, Isaiah 54:2. How do we do this, let me introduce this Name of God, -- Jehovah M'kaddesh, which means the one who sanctifies me. (I Thessalonians 5:23, I Timothy 4:5, Hebrews 2:11) Here is what I Thessalonians 5:23, says "And the very God of peace, (Jehovah Shalom) sanctify (Jehovah M'Kaddesh) you wholly(completely); and I pray God your whole spirit (all) and soul (all) and body (all) be preserved (El Shaddai) blameless (Jehovah Elohim (Lord God of Relationships)) unto the coming of our Lord Jesus Christ (Jehovah Shammah (God who is present)).

Do you remember what was wrong with the above picture?

(Hint: Door is jammed. Window sags because foundation has shifted, and is unlevel because foundation shifted). Now look at the picture on the next page.

(c) Patricia E. Adams

Terms of Contract for Sale

Opt. A) As is 100k, fix 100,000 up yourself, owner finances; or best offer

Opt. B) As is 100k, See Owner finance, you fix

Opt. C) Move in – 98k, owner makes minor repairs

Negotiable

Okay, the picture paints hopefully, words in your mind! Now notice the last thing under terms is negotiable. If the buyer does not ask the owner what they mean, will the owner tell them? Suppose you are the buyer? And you are, you have inherited a house from your parents, and it is the one you are presently living in as a spirit living in a body, with a soul having a supernatural experience in the earth.

Let's pretend that you are seeking from within the marketplace a new home, and you spot the first house in the picture, it is in a good part of town, conveniently located and nice yard, with room for expansion, but the house itself needs much work.

Which of you has the mindset to buy this house and fix it up, because you love a challenge, and which of you have no intentions of buying someone else's headaches, and which of you would be tempted to consider the options for the fun of it! Don't raise your hand, just make a mental note to yourself, and let's move on.

Negotiable means that the owner really doesn't want to sell you the house as it is, but if you don't inquire he will feel obligated to sell you the house as it is. *Here is what the owner is thinking*, (if they tell me that they would rather I make the repairs before they move in, and pay a slightly higher price for the house, I am willing (102,000). Or they want me to make the repairs after they move in, and pay a higher price of (105,000). Even, if they would only ask me, I will make all the repairs before they move in and sell the house for 98,000).

Gives us something to think about while we choose! Well this is how God sees us, we have inherited a house by birth from our parents, and the environment has worn the house for good or bad, our parents are no longer living in this house with us. It too is a great little fixer upper. But are we ready to invite company over.

We locate the fixer upper house and it looks familiar, by all the outward signs of wear and tear on it, and we are interested, because it does look better than the houses in our neighborhood. It presents us with an opportunity to try putting down roots in different soil, and a different area of town. But the repairs, well, really need to be done, but it does have room for me to move in, and work on it as I go. How many of you have seen the movie "The Money Pit" with Tom Hanks, well if you have you get the picture.

Say my house is in need of additional repair, from things that are not quite so visible, things like mildew, termites, and loose planks in the floor, and I haven't inquired of the person who holds my mortgage if I can finance these repairs, or will they pay for the repairs without cost.

You see the Bible, says we have been bought with a price, and we are not our own, therefore, God is my owner, and His Son holds the title deed. When two people come together to negotiate the terms of moving in, they each bring a house to the table, and the two become a home. I will say this again, each has a house, and the two put their houses together in spirit, and flesh and they become one home.

My question to you is this, have the necessary repairs been made in your life, which will not cause major inconveniences for your merge?

When we marry another individual we move our houses in together and make a home.

God is standing at the door of our houses and wants to merge with us and make a home, an abode with us! The tools required to make the necessary repairs, to help us sort out all the stuff we don't need and should not bring into our home. Changing our sub-standard housing into prime real estate that will support the merged contents and provide refuge from the elements, and hold up during future renovations and expansions is what God wants us as vessels of honor.

Many of us would not move into a dilapidated or condemned natural house but we will move into a sub-standard relationship in a heartbeat.

Enlarge your tent, and pace off the ground you want to possess. (Isaiah 54:2, Isaiah 61:7) (See Chapter on enlarging your Tent (Obedience))

Allow God to make you again another vessel according to Jeremiah 18. We begin this by exchanging our wills and relinquishing ownership to God, through Jesus Christ as our Lord!

> *"It is time to take back what the Devil has stolen from us as sons and daughters of our Heavenly Father. Come to ourselves like the Prodigal Son and be reconciled, restored and fitted for our royal garments. Even like David who rejected the use of a borrowed anointing by using Sauls' armor to fight the giant philistine Goliath. God has ours tailor made to fit us all over."*
>
> *Patricia E. Adams*

CHAPTER 12
♥
NOW WHAT?

"Satan, is the author of confusion and destruction."

Patricia E. Adams

Now What

12 – Now What

Changing the Guard

(Lordship)

Is and has God, through his Son Jesus Christ the Anointed One and His Anointing become Lord and Savior of your life? How do you discern when this has happened? Well, as Paul said, it is no longer I but, Christ that lives in me (Gal. 2:20). But the comforter, which is the Holy Spirit, whom the father will send in my name, he shall teach you all things, and bring all things to your remembrance, whatsoever I have said unto you. He empowers us when the Holy Spirit is come upon us, and we become witnesses unto him both in Jerusalem, and in all Judaea, and in Samaria, and unto the uttermost part of the earth. (Acts 1:8) We are no longer led away by every wind and doctrine, but He has become the light unto our feet and pathway. "Howbeit when he the Holy Spirit of Truth, is come, he will guide you into all truth, for he shall not speak of himself, but whatsoever he shall hear, that shall he speak, and he will show you things to come." (John 16:13)

"He is in control, and, "While Peter thought on the vision, the Spirit said unto him, Behold, three men seek thee. Arise therefore, and get thee down, and go with them, doubting nothing: for I have sent them." (Acts 10:19-20)

When someone is in control of a situation or person, the exact thing that is desired, by the controlling person is what is usually accomplished if they have absolute or enough power over that individual or thing. Which means that when we allow God, He is and can be the operator of our souls.

"Now when they had gone throughout Phrygia and the region of Galatia, and were forbidden of the Holy Ghost (Spirit) to preach the word in Asia, After they were come to Mysia. They assayed to go into Bithynia: but the Spirit suffered them not."(Acts 16:6-7)

We receive the constrainment of God when we are in continual fellowship with the Father is interrupted when we choose to follow our natural mind, and our non-divine nature. For as many as are led by the Spirit of God, they are the Sons of God. (Romans 8:14) We are reproved that we might not be lost with the world but receive eternal life. It is through obedience to Christ, that we are endowed with the life giving properties of salvation. "For the bread of God is he which cometh down from heaven, and giveth life unto the world." (John 6:33) We see God seated on the throne of one who is one-hearted and surrendered to his Lordship! When We No Longer Want to Be In Charge:

He becomes our Guide

"Howbeit when he, the Spirit of Truth, is come he will guide you into all truth; for he shall not speak of himself; but whatsoever he shall hear, that shall he speak; and he will show you things to come." (John 16:13)

He becomes our Controller

"While Peter thought on the vision, the spirit said unto him, behold, three men seek thee. Arise, therefore, and get thee down, and go with them, doubting nothing: for I have sent them." (Acts 10:19-20)

He becomes our Operator

"Now when they had gone throughout Phrygia and the region of Galatia, and were forbidden of the Holy Spirit to preach the word in Asia, after they were come to Mysia, they assayed to go into Bithynia: but the spirit suffered them not." (Acts 16:6)

He becomes our Reprover

"For as many as are led by the Spirit of God, they are the sons of God." (Romans 8:14)

He becomes our Life Giver

"For the bread of God is He which cometh down from Heaven, and giveth life unto the world." (John 6:33)

He becomes our Truth

"If ye had known me, ye should have known my father also: and from henceforth ye know him, and have seen him." (John 14:17)

He becomes our Comforter

"And I will pray the Father, and he shall give you another Comforter, that he may abide with you forever."(John 14:16)

He becomes our Teacher

"For the Holy Spirit shall teach you in the same hour what ye ought to say." (Luke 12:12) And...

Our desires turn towards God, because our heart is no longer divided, into the past, present, future of what if or when. When the scripture speaks to us and says, now after having done all to stand, stand. (Eph. 6:13-14) As you know a house divided against itself cannot stand. Now submit our wills to God through the covenant according to Matthew 12:25-26.

Covenanting With God - (Submission)

Submission of our will to God through Jesus Christ comes as we are receivers of our flesh being circumcised, crucified and resurrected, ascended justified, and regenerated, sanctified, servants into sonship through obedience to God's word.

They that worship him, must worship him in spirit and in truth. It is only the truth that makes us free. If ye had known me, ye should have known my father also; and from henceforth ye know him, and have seen him. (John 14:17) Through the exchange we are comforted and taught.

We are no longer led away by every wind and doctrine, but He has become the light unto our feet and our pathway. Howbeit when the Holy Spirit of Truth, is come, he will guide you into all truth, for he shall not speak of himself, but whatsoever he shall hear, that shall he speak, and he will show you things to come (John 16:13), and there is no other desire than that of being renewed through the word of God.

Self-Crucifixion - Out With the Old

Self-denial is the key to our own will in exchange for God's will, and is the only way to permanently toss out the old. As we have heard, and many have read, and have been taught that it is the "Anointing" that breaks the yoke. Jesus was a spirit inhabiting a body, as a legal vehicle sent to redeem man back to the Father and restore relationship and fellowship "koinonia."

It required not ours, but HIS death, burial, resurrection and ascenscion to destroy the roadblock erected by our forefather Adam. Jesus became the second Adam, the First and the Last, that we might be able to boldly come before the throne of grace and ask for ourselves help in our time of need. We would no longer have to depend upon the sacrifices of an earthly high priest, which was fallible to gain us atonement from our sins. But he, who knew no sin became sin, and bore all of our sins on himself, that we might have a right to the tree of life, which had been desecrated by Adam and Eve through their act of disobedience.

Gethsemane

The place of restoration for us was a crushing place for Jesus. Because he was crushed he received the next installment of his anointing. This new level of anointing allowed him to endure much for the provision of Salvation. He endured the betrayal, the arrest, the false accusations, the Crown of Thorns, the Whipping of His Back, the piercing of his hands, feet and side. The piercing of his side released the Redeeming Blood and Water of the Word, which birthed the Church as a woman coming out of the side of Adam. For the purpose of this text we will examine the word Gethsemane; from the Garden of Gethsemane. The overall name means a garden. Dividing the word in two parts gives us Geth - Semane; in the Hebrew Geth is spelled Gath - meaning a press, also in Hebrew Semane is spelled Shemen - meaning oil. Collectively the word means a --

Garden of Pressed Oil

In Matthew 26:36 and Mark 14:32 the Bible records that in this garden that it is historically located across from the Kedron and at the foot of the Mount of Olives. Kedron - means a brook from a dusky place).

We must choose between our righteousness and the righteousness of Jehovah M'Kaddesh. The process of His Sanctification, just as the olive press; presses out the meat of the fruit of the olive, our flesh is pressed out by the regeneration of our spirit man until we become justified.

Justification - Spring Cleaning the Attic

When we spring clean, we first look around the room to ascertain how big of a mess the place is in, then we decide how we are going to clean up the place. We begin to imagine how we want the room to look, and envision it in its finished state. We open the unmarked cluttered boxes in the newly moved into house and rearrange them we can sit and begin to sort through what we have collected. As we go along we begin to see things from 5, 6, and 7 years ago that have wonderful or painful memories. A garbage can is pulled out and then we began tossing things away that are no longer needed into a pile and into the garbage can. Things that are no longer applicable to our current lives, or useful are discarded; hopefully.

We often find photographs of former friends, loves and spouses. We evaluate if these photos are painful or happy. If they are painful we toss or destroy the memories; and toss out outdated or damaged clothing, or irreparable things. Some throw everything away, to make room to store things in the house, back into the attic. Others will throw away what's in the attic and the house, and start anew. Think about it in terms of the amount of space we allow God to have in our houses, our spiritual bodies for God. Just because it is neatly packed away in a closet, or hung up nicely, and out of mind does not mean that it does not need to be thrown out or repaired.

God wants to fix the broken pieces of our lives (Psalms 31:12) and inhabit every nook and cranny of our living spaces (Psalms 147:3, Jeremiah 18:4). He takes the broken pieces and makes us again, when we surrender to his purpose. The Bible says to those he calls, he justifies (sanctifies) (Romans 8:30). It is the process of sanctification, through his son Jesus Christ and the power of the word of the living God that gives us the root system that causes us to become trees planted by rivers of living water.

Then what is justification to the Christian? According to Romans 8:29-30, it is God's ability to bring out of a person that which is desired, to cause him to appear righteous by fact and not by action. The Pharisees were like this, they believed their works, and attitude of holiness was the offering of sacrificial living that

God was requiring; and thus missed their Messiah. (Luke 16:15). Jesus after examining the contents of Paul's house and attic declared him righteous "He had cleansed his heart." Titus 3:5-7, he examines what we hold onto and is aware of every hidden item (sin), and awaits our willingness to cast off and lay aside the thing that holds us captive. "Much more then, being now justified by his blood, we shall be saved from wrath, through him." (Romans 5:9)

"In whom we have redemption through his blood, the forgiveness of sins, according to the riches of his grace. Wherein He hath abounded toward us all wisdom and prudence; Having made known unto the mystery of his will, according to his good pleasure which he hath purposed in himself. That in the dispensation of the fullness of times he might gather together in one all things in Christ, both which are in heaven, and which are on earth; even in him: in whom we have obtained an inheritance, being predestined according to his purpose of him who worketh all things after the counsel of his own will; that we should be to the praise of his glory, who first trusted in Christ." (Ephesians 1:7-12)

When we trust in God, with total reliance upon his ability and provisions made for us through his love, we enter into his rest and find peace. And having made peace through the blood of his cross, by him to reconcile all things unto himself; by him, I say, whether they be things in earth, or things in heaven."

(Colossians 1:20) We can increase and have all the places that the soles of our feet tread upon, and have these places become holy through regeneration.

Regeneration - Remodeling the Attic

Now that God has searched out our every part and has known our heart. It is he who has set his love upon us. (Matthew 19:28, Titus 3:5, John 3)

Before Christ we were degenerates, (meaning declined in nature, character from a former state of being; a sinner continual, which is a backslider). Having sunk to a condition below that which is normal.(Daniel 4:33-35). Nebuchadnezzar sanked to a state of abnormality when he denied God, and exalted the things in his house above the God of the entire universe and everything under the earth. He would not allow God entrance into his personal life or business affairs, or do which was right in the sight of God.

We learned in Chapter Eight that when we express anger towards God by rebelling against him, we are of the Anti-Christ. How can two walk together if they are not in agreement (James 3:3) When we agree with God we are changed, transformed progressively into his image. Therefore we are new creations and have been remodeled. Once you remodel your house, it never goes back to the original state, unless you choose to return the house to its former state.

We must progress and grow in grace to become obedient and pleasing to God, and God pleasers can not be man pleasers, but self-pleasers.

Through remodeling, we are liberated from the former things. "As for thee also, by the blood of thy covenant I have sent forth thy prisoners out of the pit wherein is no water." (Zech. 9:11) Gaining pardon from a debt that we could not pay, "But into the second went the high priest alone once every year, not without blood, which he offered for himself, and for the errors of the people; the Holy Ghost (Spirit) this signifying, that the way into the holiest of all was not yet made manifest, while as the first tabernacle was yet standing; Which was a figure for the time then present, in which were offered both gifts and sacrifices, that could not make him that did the service perfect, as pertaining to the conscience; Which stood only in meats and drinks, and divers washings, and carnal ordinances, imposed on them until the time of reformation. (Hebrews 9:7-10)

Through the washing of the water of the word, we are purified through the sanctifying power of the atoning blood of Jesus.

Sanctification - Disinfecting the House

Through sanctification (godesh/Hebrew) we are separated from the old self and set apart for a good work. (Psalms 51:7-10)

What shall separate us from his love, for with his love he has saved us. If we are separated from this love then we shall surely perish. (Romans 8:35) (See Romans 8:29)

Oftentimes, Comet, 401, Lysol and Pinesol are used when we are cleaning our houses. Most of the time when we are spring cleaning we put together a very serious combination of all, and nobody can stay in the house during or after the clean-up. Praise God, when he spring cleans our house/triune bodies it only requires the use of one thing that is all purpose to clean us up completely, and that is the "Blood of Jesus." Through the blood we have access to the kingdom of God, where we can decree a thing and it shall be done for us. The blood of Jesus entitled us to gain access/inheritance to the Keys of David, The Keys to Death, Hell, and the Grave.

The Keys of David	Rev. 3:7	Isaiah 22:22
The Keys of Hell	Rev. 1:18	
The Keys of Death	Rev. 1:18	

And provided us with the things that come from a united life of one-heartedness (unity) in Christ:

We have shelter, "And the blood shall be to you for a token upon the houses where ye are: and when I see the blood, I will pass over you, and the plague shall not be upon you to destroy you, when I smite the land of Egypt." (Exodus 12:13)

Cleansing us as we walk in the light, as he is in the light, we have fellowship one with another, and the blood of Jesus Christ his son cleanseth us from all sin. (I John 1:7) "And almost all things are by the law purged with blood; and without shedding of blood is no remission." (Hebrews 9:22) Having all things purged we have made room to enlarge our place for the soles of our feet to tread upon. Where only the obedient can walk and prosper! Walking in the promises of God that are yes and amen! We have an advocate with the Father who has enforced our rights to be heirs of the Kingdom of God and to possess the land and have dominion over everything that he has entrusted to our care and take back our territory.

Enlarging Your Tent

(Obedience)

Examples of Those Who obeyed and possessed their Souls Desires:

Hannah made room for one by fasting and prayer for a son.

Mary made room for one by presenting herself as a living sacrifice.

Boaz made room for one by commanding that provisions be laid aside for his future bride.

Ruth made room for one by accepting God as her God, and received a double portion. God made room for one through his Son Jesus, as a way of escape into sanctification

Widow Zarephath made room for one by sacrificing to the man of God, and received everlasting provisions.

Jesus made room for one by doing away with the veil, emptying himself of his glory and making himself the more excellent way for all to come unto the father.

Mary Magdalene made room by walking away from the lust of the flesh and the pride of life, to find a man who would and did love her beyond what she had experienced and gave her a feeling that was everlasting and not fleeting.

The Woman with the Issue of Blood had been bowed over and loosing her life with every step she took, as the blood coursed out of her body like water being poured from a pitcher. She knew that healing was to be had if she could touch the hem of his garment, what she needed was at his feet and not in his hand that day. The oil flowed from the head to the skirts and gathered there and in her mind, she needed all of him and nothing less to dry up the issues of her life and bring total restoration.

The Woman at the Well had many relations and no legal rights to any man, he told her what only he could tell her and she knew from that moment she had been in the presence of a man like none that she had been with before and that he was 'the man' above all that would satisfy her longings and turn her sorrow into joy. He became her husbandman.

Saul/Paul made room for one by surrendering his authority to God's authority, and received a prize far beyond measurement.

Is and has God revealing and revealed things, stuff and people in your life who have got to go?

Dr. Charles Stanley on one of his programs spoke on obedience. This is not a verbatim account but an abbreviated version, and I believe you will still get the message.

It is ours to obey and trust, and God's to respond to the consequences of our obedience and trust. He is obligated to be, His Word to supply our needs. Trust completely, no matter what the word of God is still true. Learn to wait on God's timing and direction as in Isaiah 64:4. Give generously to the Lord's work as in II Corinthians 9. We cannot live the Christian life without Christ living in us. (John 15, Galatians 2:20). God is in absolute control of every circumstance of our lives. (Romans 8:28)

Don't reject God's sovereignty, absolutely depend upon the Holy Spirit for everything. Personal time of meditation should be your time with God. Pray the scriptures, on our knees, not in tangents and fits. Ask Him what he wants us to do. (Joshua 1:6-8, 9).

Enlarging Your Tent Prayer - (Isaiah 64: 1-12)

Psalms 144:5	Phil. 3:9
Micah 1:4	Psalms 90:5-6
Exodus 34:10	Ephesians 2:10
Psalms 68:8	Psalms 74:1-2
Psalms 31:19	Psalms 79:13
I Corinthians 2:9	Psalms 79:1
Acts 10:35	Psalms 74:7
Acts 26:8	Ezekiel 24:21
Malachi 3:6	Psalms 83:1

Having therefore, brethren, boldness to enter into the holiest by the blood of Jesus, by a new and living way, which he hath consecrated for us, through the veil, that is to say, his flesh, and having an high priest over the house of God; let us draw near with a true heart in full assurance of faith, having our hearts sprinkled from an evil conscience, and our bodies washed with pure water. (Hebrews 10:19-22).

The sealer of promise (The Holy Spirit) to everlasting life authorizes us to use the keys of knowledge, binding and loosing. We become inhabitable and prepared to be cohabitants with Christ and our future and present spouses and families.

Binding: Matthew 16:19, and

Loosing: Matthew 18:18

God will answer your prayer based on the following scriptures:

Isaiah 65:1-25	Romans 9:24
Ephesians 2:12	Romans 10:21
Deuteronomy 32:21	Leviticus 17:15
Deuteronomy 18:11	Matthew 9:11
Luke 18:11	Judges 19
Hosea 9:12	Revelations 21:1
Zephaniah 1:5	I Kings 8:27
II Chronicles 6:18	Matthew 5:34
Genesis 3:14	

The Lord's Prayer is our model, and it directs us to Adore Him, Seek his divine intervention, Submit to his will, He will give us our needs, we are Required to forgive, and He guides us into deliverance, so that his kingdom and his power and his glory will be performed in us and in the earth as it is in heaven. So that we might walk in righteousness, joy and peace in the Holy Ghost (Matthew 6:13b).

Cleansed and Salted - Ezekiel 16:4

How come only one in ten people, who make a commitment to Christ, are still serving Him 5 years later? Ezekiel gives us some answers:

(1) We must be washed! Your spiritual protection against dirt, disease, and death is "the washing of water by the Word" (Ephesians 5:26). It's not enough to step into the shower every morning " you've also got to step into the Scriptures. Jesus said, Now are ye clean through the word" (Jn 15:3). Sin will keep you from your Bible, and your Bible will keep you from sin.

(2)We must be salted! In Hebrew culture, they rubbed salt on newborn babies to toughen their skins so that they could be handled without bruising. Too many of us need "special handling." We're touchy. If we're corrected, we get defensive. Only when you've been "salted" by mature love and non-legalistic acceptance, can you be really open and honest.

(3) We must be swaddled! When we're born into God's family, we're vulnerable and need o be covered and protected. This is the value of Christian fellowship; it wraps you up tightly in the arms of love and says, "You don't ever have to go back to the old life again! You can begin afresh., be healed of your painful past, have good times and good relationships instead of bad ones." Believers, have we been washed, salted, and swaddled?

CHAPTER 13

THROUGH SANCTIFICATION

Through Sanctification

13 – Through Sanctification – Jehovah M'Kaddesh

(Marilyn Hickey, excerpted from the Names of God, pp. 98,106,109,110)

"Have you ever had a strong desire to have your personality to line up perfectly with the Lord's personality? Jesus wants you to have a total image of Himself living through you. He gives you that image in the name Jehovah M'Kaddesh ...first found in Leviticus 20:7,8... many Christians drift here and wander there --not really knowing God's plan for them.

They know about the possibility of having a deeper relationship with Him, and they know about the baptism of the

Holy Spirit, and some even may be baptized in the Holy Spirit, but there seems to be no growth, nor a real hunger for growth...It is because there is something lacking, and the key is in the name Jehovah M'Kaddesh...it is the way in which the revealing One would have his people walk... to **sanctify means to consecrate, to dedicate, or to become holy**...being set apart...to walk in total dedication to Him...everything the Jewish people did in the Bible, and today all relate back to their God...God did not do all of the sanctifying...within the name

Jehovah M'Kaddesh will not allow us to believe a lie, but tell us **the truth that men must choose holiness** ....Nebuchadnezzar's spirit came in line with the Lord. What happened? **His mind, intellect, reasoning, and physical body changed from being like an animal's. He became a man of God**...I Thes. 4:3,...**talks about keeping your entire spirit, soul, and body blameless...God doesn't want you to have little hidden closets and missed motivations.**

How do you sanctify yourself? ...relying **totally on Him in Everything!**

Jehovah M'Kaddesh appears over 700 times...because God wants a people who are set apart unto Him...When you belong to God, you have been set apart...not in flesh...mind...alone won't cut it...you must be set apart to serve Him in spirit and in truth!

God called Jonah to prophesy to Nineveh...Jonah had a problem...he had mixed motivations...He wanted to obey God's call only when it suited him. Although he loved God with all of his mind, his spirit was not set apart...Jonah had some time to think things over, inside of the grave within a seemingly bottomless pit (fish). He totally consecrated himself, spirit and all, unto the Lord God (this is a prophecy in symbolism, that foretold the death, burial, and time in hell to accomplish the resurrection of us all, through Christ Jesus).

Unlike Jonah, who even after he obeyed, returned to the way he was before... Because his spirit had not been sanctified....for I the Lord your God am holy...the word **"holiness" confuses many people, but...**think of it this way: **when you set yourself apart unto God, you will be whole -** you will be holy... He just wants us **complete,** starting with our spirits...when it is in right relationship with God, your soul and body will line up...your soul and body are just **things that your spirit wears. Holiness, is a setting apart, that begins with the wholeness of God inside of you.**

Every **7th** year is the Year of Jubilee, after the children of Israel had observed the solemn fasting and feasting; after having set apart themselves, and everything they had in their possessions for 7 Sabbath moons. (Which were times of honoring the Lord for his continual care).

The 7th year was ushered in, redemption proclaimed, and liberty for all who were in bondage, is celebrated the entire year. Is this the seventh year approaching US and perhaps passed as you are reading this book.

ARE YOU READY!!! If not GET OUT OF MY WAY!!! I AM COMING THROUGH!!!

What hinders you that you can not run? (read Galatians 5:7)

And be ready, to celebrate the Year of Jubilee, symbolically this can be yours everyday, we do not have to wait for the annual fasting and feasting. Because a more excellent way has been prepared through Christ Jesus, so that you may have Jubilee every day, moment, and second of your life.

MAY BLESSING, AND HONOR BE HIS!!!

Endnotes

MATERIALS
Bibles: King James Version

Books:
Myles Munroe, copyright 1991
Single, Married, Separated & Life After Divorce
Bahamas Faith Ministries Published by Vincom, Inc.
P.O. Box 702400
Tulsa, OK 74170
Reprint Permission Granted by Vincom, Inc.

Eugenia Price
Woman to Woman, copyright 1959
Zondervan Books
Zondervan Publishing House
Grand Rapids, MI 49506
Used by Permission of Zondervan Publishing House

Derek and Ruth Prince
God Is A Matchmaker, 1986
Chosen Books a Division of Baker Book House
P.O. Box 6287
Grand Rapids, MI 49516-6287
Used by Permission of Baker Book House

Spiros Zodhiates
The Complete Word Study – New Testament
Chattanooga, TN 37422
AMG Publishers, 1991
6815 Shallowford Rd.
Box 22000
Reprint Permission Granted by AMG Publishers

Other Volumes in the One Heart Series

VOLUME 1
With Oneness of Heart
ISBN 0-9700976-0-3
Formats: Paper, Audio, E-Book & Digital, Kindle
 Book: Disciple's Guide
 Audio: Disciple's Overview

VOLUME 2
Book: Journeying to the Road Called Oneness
ISBN 0-9700976-1-1
Formats: Paper, Audio, E-Book & Digital, Kindle
 Book: Disciple's Guide
 Audio: Disciple's Overview

VOLUME 3
Detouring off the Road of Oneness
ISBN 0-9700976-2-X
Formats: Paper, Audio, E-Book & Digital, Kindle
 Book: Disciple's Guide
 Audio: Disciple's Overview

VOLUME 4
I and My Father Are One
ISBN 0-9700976-3-8
Formats: Paper, Audio, E-Book & Digital, Kindle
 Book: Disciple's Guide
 Audio: Disciple's Overview

VOLUME 5
52 Week Devotional & Journal Study/Application
ISBN 09700976-7-0
Formats: Paperback

Website: www.oneheartseries.com
Affiliate Program: www.oneheartseriesaffiliates.com
Radio Network: www.oneheartsoundmedianetwork.com
Email: author@oneheartseries.com

www.ingramcontent.com/pod-product-compliance
Lightning Source LLC
Chambersburg PA
CBHW060954230426
43665CB00015B/2194